COIN COLLECTING FOR BEGINNERS

THE MOST UP-TO-DATE GUIDE TO START YOUR WORLD COIN COLLECTION, MASTER COIN IDENTIFICATION, UNDERSTAND VALUATION TECHNIQUES, PRESERVE YOUR TREASURES AND MAXIMIZE PROFITS

SPENCER REED

© **Copyright 2024 Spencer Reed - All rights reserved.**

The content contained within this book may not be reproduced, duplicated or transmitted without direct written permission from the author or the publisher.

Under no circumstances will any blame or legal responsibility be held against the publisher, or author, for any damages, reparation, or monetary loss due to the information contained within this book, either directly or indirectly.

Legal Notice:

This book is copyright protected. It is only for personal use. You cannot amend, distribute, sell, use, quote or paraphrase any part, or the content within this book, without the consent of the author or publisher.

Disclaimer Notice:

Please note the information contained within this document is for educational and entertainment purposes only. All effort has been executed to present accurate, up to date, reliable, complete information. No warranties of any kind are declared or implied. Readers acknowledge that the author is not engaged in the rendering of legal, financial, medical or professional advice. The content within this book has been derived from various sources. Please consult a licensed professional before attempting any techniques outlined in this book.

By reading this document, the reader agrees that under no circumstances is the author responsible for any losses, direct or indirect, that are incurred as a result of the use of the information contained within this document, including, but not limited to, errors, omissions, or inaccuracies.

TABLE OF CONTENTS

Introduction	7
1. DELVING INTO THE WORLD OF COIN COLLECTING	13
What Is a Coin?	14
Coin Collecting and Numismatics	18
Brief History of Coin Collecting	20
Why Do People Collect Coins?	22
Summary	24
Conclusion	25
2. SETTING YOUR GOALS AND ASSEMBLING YOUR TOOLKIT	27
Setting Your Coin Collecting Goals	28
Setting SMART Goals	33
Tracking Your Progress and Adjusting Goals	36
Considering Budgetary Constraints	37
Gathering the Essential Tools for Coin Collecting	39
Summary	42
Conclusion	43
3. MASTERING COIN IDENTIFICATION	45
Exploring Coin Anatomy and Terminology	46
Understanding Different Types of Coins	52
Utilizing Technology for Coin Identification	61
Summary	62
Conclusion	63
4. UNDERSTANDING THE MINTING PROCESS	65
What Is a Mint?	66
The Process of Coin Design	70
The Process of US Coin Production	72
The Process of Coin Circulation	76
Summary	78
Conclusion	80

5. SOURCING YOUR COINS WISELY … 85
   Identifying Sources for Coins … 86
   Finding Trusted Sources … 88
   Verifying Coin Authenticity … 90
   Protecting Yourself … 94
   Summary … 96
   Conclusion … 98

   Quiz … 99

6. NAVIGATING COIN GRADING … 109
   Importance of Coin Grading … 110
   Grading Standards and Systems … 112
   Top Grading Services … 115
   How to Grade a Coin … 117
   Building Your Grading Skills … 119
   Summary … 121
   Conclusion … 122

7. DETERMINING THE WORTH OF YOUR COIN … 123
   Importance of Coin Valuation … 124
   Factors Influencing Coin Value … 125
   How to Determine Coin Value … 127
   Summary … 136
   Conclusion … 136

8. HANDLING AND CLEANING COINS SAFELY … 139
   Handling Coins Properly … 140
   Best Practices for Handling Coins … 141
   Why You Should Not Clean Coins … 142
   Cleaning Coins Safely … 144
   Understanding Coin Damage … 146
   Coin Damage or Mint Errors? … 147
   What to Do With Damaged Coins … 149
   Summary … 151
   Conclusion … 152

9. STORING AND ORGANIZING YOUR COIN COLLECTION … 153
   Importance of Proper Storage … 154
   Choosing the Right Storage Environment … 156

Considerations for Choosing Coin Storage	158
Maintaining Organization and Accessibility	161
Implementing Security Measures	163
Summary	164
Conclusion	166
10. EXPLORING PROFIT OPPORTUNITY	**167**
The Potential for Profit	168
Strategies for Profit Maximization	170
How to Sell Your Coins	173
Tax Considerations	176
Summary	177
Conclusion	178
Conclusion	181
Quiz	185
References	195
Image References	203

INTRODUCTION

In a world that often looks forward, my intrigue was captured by something decidedly from the past, nestled within my palm—the intricate world of coins. This journey didn't start in grandeur but with a simple, yet profound, gift from my grandfather: his coin collection. It was a collection steeped in history, each piece a memento from his time spent traveling the world with the military. My grandfather began collecting coins during his service, each one from a different country he was stationed in, representing both a reminder of his experiences and a tangible link to the diverse cultures he encountered. That gift did more than just start a hobby; it ignited a passion, turning me into both a guardian and a storyteller of history's physical tokens.

My fascination with coins wasn't driven by financial gain or public acclaim but by a genuine interest in the stories they held. What began as a childhood curiosity has deepened into a professional pursuit. The more I delved into numismatics—the study and collection of currency, including coins, tokens, paper money, and related objects—the more I recognized its power to connect us with the economic, cultural, and political currents of our ancestors.

This dedication to coin collecting has taken me from quiet hours spent over books and coins to lively exchanges at international coin shows. Each coin, with its design and marks of wear, is a chapter in a much larger story—one that spans across civilizations and ages.

At the core of my passion is the compelling narrative each coin offers—tales of empires risen and fallen, of economic revolutions, and of the endless human quest for beauty and value. It is this narrative that I seek to share through my writing. I aim to simplify the complex world of numismatics, making it accessible to everyone from the curious novice to the seasoned collector. My writing mirrors my journey: fueled by enthusiasm, anchored in expertise, and always respectful of the history and legacy each coin carries.

Navigating the world of coin collecting can indeed be daunting. With an abundance of information available, it's not uncommon to encounter sources that are outdated, complex, or biased, which can make your journey feel overwhelming. The excitement of uncovering a rare coin is often balanced by concerns over authenticity, the intricacies of verification, and the necessities of proper care. Moreover, as you look to grow your collection or assess its worth, you might find yourself facing numerous hurdles.

Coin collecting is much more than just gathering pieces of metal; it's a bridge to the rich tapestry of human history, offering insights into the economic, cultural, and political narratives of different eras. *Coin Collecting for Beginners* carefully guides you through the essentials, teaching you how to identify and value various coins, and advancing to more complex preservation techniques that enhance both their historical and financial value. The book thoroughly explains the importance of coin grading, handling, and strategic acquisition, emphasizing careful and informed collecting to avoid the common pitfalls like damage due to improper storage or handling.

In managing your coin collection, the book highlights the critical need for proper storage solutions that protect your coins from environmental damage and ensure their long-term preservation. It advises on the best materials that won't chemically react with your coins, such as acid-free paper and inert metals for cases. You'll also learn effective methods to organize and catalog your collection, making sure each coin's history and condition are accurately documented. This not only helps maintain the collection's value and historical integrity but also boosts its appeal whether kept privately or displayed publicly.

As you progress you'll discover strategies to transform your hobby into a financial venture. It offers detailed insights on how to navigate coin shows, auctions, and online platforms for buying and selling coins, emphasizing the need to understand market dynamics and spot undervalued coins that could offer significant returns. This comprehensive guide doesn't just increase your knowledge and enjoyment of coin collecting; it also empowers you to make informed, strategic decisions that can substantially enhance the value of your collection. By the end of the book, you'll not only grasp the basics and complexities of coin collecting but also appreciate the profound historical and cultural significance of numismatics.

Your decision to explore coin collecting is more than just a hobby; it's a journey into history and craftsmanship, guided by the allure of uncovering the stories behind each coin. Perhaps it was an inherited collection, an intriguing coin you found, or a fascination with history that drew you in. This initial spark has led you to seek out knowledge and deepen your understanding of numismatics, recognizing the value and significance of coins beyond their monetary worth.

Coin Collecting for Beginners is crafted to support your ambition to enhance your skills in coin collecting, regardless of your starting point. The book is designed to provide you with a comprehensive foundation in the essentials—from identifying and valuing coins to preserving them for future generations. You'll find straightforward, actionable advice that demystifies the complex aspects of numismatics, making the hobby accessible and enjoyable.

This guide presents an opportunity to connect with the historical and cultural significance of coins, offering insights into the craftsmanship that goes into each piece. In the chapters ahead, you'll gain a solid grasp of numismatics, starting with the core skill of coin identification and extending to understanding the minting process. You'll learn how to judiciously source coins, comprehend the details of coin grading, and accurately assess the value of your collection. Further on, practical advice awaits on the proper handling and cleaning of coins, methods for efficient storage and organization, and insights into turning your collecting into potential financial gain.

You'll emerge with the confidence to identify, value, and preserve your growing collection. Step by step, you'll navigate the once murky waters of numismatics, now clear with the insights and guidance contained within these pages. By the conclusion of this book, you will have mastered the art of coin collecting, understanding not just the what and the how, but the why.

In *Coin Collecting for Beginners*, my aim is to smooth out the steep learning curve that I once climbed, designed to steer you clear of common mistakes and toward informed decisions. It's the book for you if you're seeking a clear, authoritative path into the rewarding world of coin collecting, fortified by the wisdom of a seasoned collector. Here, I've laid out a path free from the brambles of uncertainty, where every step forward is a step toward a more knowledgeable, confident future in numismatics.

Now that you've started to think about the history, the intricacies, and the true art behind each coin in your collection we turn our attention to Chapter One. Here, we begin a more detailed exploration of coin collecting. You'll learn about the essential tools and insights required to start or enhance your collection. Whether you're driven by the potential for investment, the pleasure of the hobby, or the satisfaction of historical preservation, the next chapters will serve as your practical guide. They're designed to provide you with the knowledge you need to approach coin collecting with assurance and skill. Let's step forward into your step-by-step guide to navigating this timeless pursuit with confidence and expertise.

1

DELVING INTO THE WORLD OF COIN COLLECTING

Coin collecting is often misunderstood. Some people think it's too expensive or that it's becoming less popular. However, these ideas don't capture the whole picture. Let's clear up these misconceptions and show how coin collecting is an accessible and thriving hobby.

Firstly, it's not true that you need a lot of money to collect coins. While some rare coins are costly, many others are not. You can start by looking at the coins you come across every day or by finding affordable pieces that interest you (Jones, 2024). The real joy of collecting isn't in spending a lot of money, but in finding coins that have meaning or history that you appreciate.

Secondly, coin collecting isn't a dying hobby. In fact, it's gaining popularity (Passy, 2021). Thanks to the internet and social media, it's easier than ever for collectors to share their passion, buy and sell coins, and learn from each other. This means more people are discovering the excitement of finding that special coin to add to their collection.

In this chapter we're going to explore what makes a coin special beyond its value in money. We'll look at what coins are made of, what features they have, and why they're important pieces of history. Coins tell stories about the places and times they come from, and collecting them lets us hold a piece of that history in our hands.

Coin collecting is for everyone. Whether you have a lot of money to spend or just a little, and whether you're just starting out or you've been collecting for years, there's always something new to discover. Let's enter the fascinating world of coins and see what we can find.

WHAT IS A COIN?

A coin can be defined as a small, round piece of metal that is officially issued by a government as money and carries a certain value, which is recognized for transactions within and sometimes outside the issuing country (*What Is a Coin?*, 2023).

When you delve into the specifics of what constitutes a coin, there are essential features that distinguish it from other objects. These include the name of the issuing country, the value of the coin (denomination), and the date of issuance. These details are vital because they authenticate the coin as a legitimate part of a nation's currency.

The word "exonumia" encompasses all numismatic items or objects similar to coins that do not have the status of legal currency. For example, this category includes tokens used in subway systems, which, while they serve a specific monetary function within a confined environment, are not recognized as official money.

Coins are more than just monetary instruments; they are also historical artifacts. The earliest known coins were made in the kingdom of Lydia around the 7th century BCE. They were made of electrum, a natural alloy of gold and silver, and often bore the images of lions or bulls. Coins have since evolved to feature various designs and have been made of numerous materials, including copper, silver, gold, and nickel (*The Anatomy of a Coin*, 2018).

Today's coins are typically composed of metal alloys and are produced in a facility known as a mint. The design of a coin typically includes an obverse (the front or "heads" side), which may feature a notable individual or emblem, and a reverse (the back or "tails" side), which may display culturally or historically significant imagery.

The edge of a coin is its third side, sometimes adorned with grooves (reeding) or inscriptions. The rim is a raised boundary that protects the coin's design from wear and gives the coin its distinctive shape. The field is the flat, unadorned surface that allows the raised elements, known as the relief, to stand out. This relief includes the coin's devices (the main design elements), legends (inscriptions), and other markings like mint marks, which indicate where the coin was produced.

In contemporary monetary systems, coins typically represent lower denominations, while higher values are denoted by banknotes. While the digital economy has transformed financial transactions, coins remain a crucial element of trade and commerce, particularly for small-value transactions.

Historical Significance

The evolution of coins from ancient to modern times offers a fascinating glimpse into the history of civilization, commerce, and culture. Initially, as human societies transitioned from nomadic lifestyles to settled communities, the complexity of trade increased, necessitating a departure from the cumbersome barter system. The invention of coins, dating back to the 5th or 6th century BCE, marked a pivotal moment in economic history, streamlining trade and laying the foundation for the complex financial systems we see today (*The History of Coins*, n.d.).

The genesis of coinage is a topic of historical intrigue, with the first coins believed to have appeared around 600 B.C. in Lydia, an ancient kingdom in what is now Turkey. As mentioned above, these early coins were made from electrum, a natural alloy of gold and silver, and featured the stylized head of a lion. This innovation not only facilitated trade but also represented a profound shift in societal organization and economic activity, fostering a new way of thinking about value and exchange (Whipps, 2007).

Simultaneously, ancient China was also developing its form of currency, initially using cowrie shells during the Shang Dynasty before transitioning to metal coins. These early Chinese coins, distinguished by their square or round holes for easy transport, underscore the global parallel development of coinage as a solution to the inefficiencies of barter.

The Romans, around 27 B.C., further advanced the concept of currency by establishing a system where the value of a coin was determined by its denomination rather than its weight in precious metals. This development toward fiat money enabled the Roman Empire to expand its economic influence but also laid the groundwork for potential devaluation and inflation, issues still relevant in modern economies.

As coinage evolved, so did the methods of production, from hand-hammered coins in ancient times to the sophisticated machine-struck coins of the Industrial Revolution. This technological advancement facilitated the mass production of coins, meeting the increasing demand for currency in burgeoning industrial societies.

COIN COLLECTING AND NUMISMATICS

Coin collecting is the art of accumulating coins from various periods or countries, driven by historical, educational, or personal enjoyment motives. This hobby, engaging enthusiasts for centuries, offers a tangible connection to the past, showcasing the evolution of economies, art, and cultures through the metal pieces used as currency.

At its core, coin collecting is about the appreciation of coins as more than mere mediums of transaction. Collectors often pursue pieces based on specific criteria such as country of origin, time period, mint marks, or themes. This can include collecting coins from every country, focusing on a particular era like the Roman Empire or the medieval period, or even gathering coins with errors or unique minting flaws (Jobes, 2022). The variety within coin collecting is vast, with collectors choosing paths that resonate with their interests or investment strategies.

The hobby not only enriches one's understanding of history but also fosters a sense of community among collectors. Engaging in forums, clubs, and shows, collectors share insights, trade coins, and celebrate new discoveries, thus contributing to a vibrant, knowledge-rich community.

Educationally, coin collecting opens a window to the economic systems, artistic endeavors, and societal changes of various eras. Through their collections, enthusiasts gain insights into the design and composition of coins, including the metals used and the reasons behind their adoption. For instance, the transition from precious metals like gold and silver to base metals in coinage reflects economic and technological shifts over time.

Moreover, the hobby can be an investment. The value of coins can appreciate based on rarity, condition, and historical significance. Collectors might find joy in unearthing a coin that not only adds aesthetic value to their collection but also holds potential financial gain. The thrill of the hunt for these valuable pieces adds an exciting dimension to coin collecting, blending passion with profit.

Numismatics

Numismatics refers to the detailed study of coins, which is a step beyond simply collecting them. Although all numismatists collect coins, not everyone who collects coins engages in this level of study.

Coin collectors aim to complete sets based on specific criteria such as date, mintmark, denomination, or country of origin. Their collection can be highly structured, aiming for completeness in a certain category, or more personal, holding onto coins that carry individual significance without necessarily focusing on the completion of sets.

Numismatists, on the other hand, delve into the study and understanding of coins and money from historical, social, and artistic perspectives (*What's the Difference Between Being a*

Numismatist & a Coin Collector?, 2018). Their engagement with coins is not just about accumulation but includes extensive research into various aspects of coins and currency. This could involve specializing in certain areas like Lincoln cents or Canadian coins, writing about coins, or studying the vast amount of literature available on the subject. Numismatists might also seek to discover new varieties of coin designs, errors, and other numismatic curiosities.

BRIEF HISTORY OF COIN COLLECTING

Coin collecting has evolved significantly through the ages as it is deeply intertwined with history, culture, and society. Here's an overview of its journey through key historical periods, notable collectors, and pivotal events that have shaped this enduring pastime.

Ancient Greece and Rome

The roots of coin collecting trace back to the ancient civilizations of Greece and Rome, where coins were not only currency but also works of art and political propaganda. The hobby is believed to be nearly as old as coinage itself, with evidence suggesting that even emperors like Augustus (reigned 27 BC–AD 14) collected old and foreign coins, appreciating them beyond their monetary value (Sayles, 2024).

Medieval and Renaissance Europe

Coin collecting gained a more systematic approach during the Medieval period, continuing into the Renaissance. Notably, Petrarch (1304–1374), a figure of the Italian Renaissance, is known for his scientific collection of ancient coins, indicating a shift toward collecting for historical and artistic value rather than just economic (Sayles, 2024). This period also saw the emergence of coin collecting among the elite, with nobility and scholars using coins to complement their knowledge of classical history. The Medici family and the Habsburgs were among the prominent collectors, with large numismatic collections indicating the prestige and cultural significance of the hobby.

Modern and Contemporary World

The modern era witnessed the democratization of coin collecting, expanding beyond the realms of royalty and the affluent to the general public. The 19th and 20th centuries, in particular, saw a significant increase in interest, partly due to industrialization and the rise of the middle class. Numismatic societies were founded, and coin collecting became a widespread hobby. Notable figures such as Thomas Jefferson, John Quincy Adams, and even artists like Goethe and Winckelmann engaged in the hobby, underscoring its broad appeal (*Coin Collecting*, 2016).

The establishment of numismatic societies and the advent of coin magazines and journals further fueled interest in the hobby, making it more accessible to a wider audience. The hobby also benefitted from the professionalization of the field, with coin dealers and auctions playing a vital role in the circulation and acquisition of collectible coins.

In recent times, coin collecting has embraced the digital age, with the internet offering new platforms for collectors to buy, sell, and share knowledge about coins. Enthusiasts now have unprecedented access to coins through online platforms. This has both expanded the hobby to a global audience and introduced new challenges, including issues related to authenticity and the preservation of cultural heritage.

Coin collecting is looking up, thanks to a mix of traditional appreciation and new technology. Now, with third-party grading, online auctions, and marketplaces, it's easier for new collectors to get involved. There's a growing interest in both new and old coins, showing that the hobby is thriving and changing. Young people are still getting into coin collecting, proving it's not a dying hobby (McMorrow-Hernandez, 2019).

WHY DO PEOPLE COLLECT COINS?

People collect coins for different reasons. Coin collecting lets you see into the past and present, mixing history, art, investing, personal satisfaction, and family heritage into one interesting hobby.

Historical Fascination

Have you ever held a coin and wondered about its journey through time? Consider the awe of holding an Indian head cent from 1883, marveling at its historical journey (*Why Do You Collect Coins?*, 2004). Or think about using coins to bond with family over shared stories and history, teaching younger generations about their heritage. Coin collecting offers a unique window into the past, connecting us to the broader narrative of human civilization through tangible pieces of history.

Artistic Appreciation

Coins are more than just currency; they're miniature works of art. Many collectors are drawn to the beauty and craftsmanship of coins like the Saint-Gaudens double eagle, celebrated for its stunning design (Bucki, 2021). Appreciating coins goes beyond their monetary value, offering a glimpse into the cultural and historical contexts that shaped their creation. It's about seeing the artistry in metal and understanding the stories behind each design.

Investment Potential

Imagine discovering a coin, maybe something like a 1775 silver Spanish reale, which you picked up for just $3, only to find out it's now worth over $80 (*Why Do You Collect Coins?*, 2004). That's the kind of story that lights up the world of coin collecting. It's not just about holding onto history but also about the chance to see your collection grow in value over time. The thrill of uncovering coins with both historical significance and investment potential can turn coin collecting into a rewarding financial journey.

Relaxation and the Thrill of the Hunt

For many, coin collecting is a relaxing hobby that brings excitement and satisfaction. Whether you're searching for that rare find in your change or completing a specific collection, the hunt is an addictive part of the hobby. It's the joy of the chase and the sense of accomplishment when you finally find that elusive piece. This pursuit offers a unique blend of relaxation and excitement, making coin collecting a deeply fulfilling activity.

Legacy Building and Family Tradition

Coin collecting can create a lasting legacy, passing from one generation to the next. Imagine inheriting a cherished collection from a grandparent, a collection filled with stories and history. It's more than just collecting coins; it's about preserving a tangible link to your past and keeping your family's history alive. Coin collections become treasured family heirlooms, fostering connections and continuing traditions through generations.

SUMMARY

- **Accessibility of Coin Collecting:** Contrary to common misconceptions, coin collecting is not an exclusively expensive hobby. Individuals can start collecting with

everyday coins or affordable pieces that hold personal significance, emphasizing the hobby's accessibility to people with different budgets.
- **Growing Popularity:** Coin collecting is not a declining hobby but is actually gaining popularity. The advent of the internet and social media has made it easier for enthusiasts to connect, share, trade, and enhance their knowledge, contributing to the hobby's expanding community.
- **Educational and Historical Value:** Coins are not just monetary items but also carry immense historical and cultural significance. They offer insights into the history, art, and technological advancements of the societies from which they originate, making coin collecting an educational pursuit.
- **Diverse Interests and Community:** Coin collecting caters to a wide range of interests, whether it be collecting coins from specific countries, eras, or based on unique features. This diversity fosters a vibrant and supportive community of collectors who share knowledge and experiences.
- **Investment and Legacy:** Beyond the pleasure of collecting, coins can also represent a form of investment, with the potential for certain items to appreciate in value over time. Furthermore, coin collections often become cherished family heirlooms, passing historical knowledge and personal narratives across generations.

CONCLUSION

As we conclude the beginning of our exploration of coin collecting, we've discovered that this pastime is much more than simply accumulating coins. It's a deeply enriching activity that's open to everyone, challenging the misconception that it's reserved for a select few. The advent of the digital era has significantly broadened this community, enabling collectors to effortlessly share and gain knowledge.

Throughout this chapter, we've come to appreciate that coins are far more than just means of transaction; they are historical treasures and pieces of art that narrate the tales of ancient societies. The world of coin collecting is inviting to all, offering an opportunity to connect with history and art, and the exciting possibility of uncovering valuable finds.

Moving forward, the next chapter will offer actionable tips to further your journey in coin collecting. From establishing precise objectives to budget management, we plan to provide you with the tools needed to make coin collecting a fulfilling aspect of your life.

2

SETTING YOUR GOALS AND ASSEMBLING YOUR TOOLKIT

Embarking on the journey of coin collecting involves entering a realm of discovery and preservation, much like the pursuits of a seasoned archaeologist. Picture yourself setting out with a sense of purpose, equipped with knowledge and an eye for detail, ready to explore the vast expanse of numismatics. Your mission is both thrilling and meaningful—to uncover coins that have been minted through the ages, each with its own story to tell. These coins are not merely pieces of metal but are treasures that encapsulate moments of history, showcasing exquisite artistry and inherent value.

Like an archaeologist who meticulously plans their digs, understanding the significance of each artifact, a coin collector approaches their hobby with deliberation and the right tools. Establishing clear goals sets a course that leads to a meaningful and enjoyable collection. Whether your interest lies in ancient Roman coins, the intricate designs of modern decimal pieces, or the coins from specific historical periods or regions, having clear targets helps to focus your efforts, choose your coins wisely, and build a collection that reflects your personal tastes and interests.

SETTING YOUR COIN COLLECTING GOALS

Setting clear goals for your coin collection helps guide you through your numismatic journey. By having specific aims, you can focus your efforts, choose your coins wisely, and keep a clear direction for your collection.

Guiding Your Collecting Journey: By setting clear goals, you'll find it easier to navigate the broad and fascinating world of coin collecting. Whether you're drawn to medieval European coins, rare mint errors, specific historical periods like the Georgian era, or coins from regions like Asia, having specific targets helps make your collecting journey more meaningful and enjoyable. It allows you to focus on what truly interests you, leading to a collection that reflects your personal tastes and interests (*Coin Collecting Guide*, n.d.).

Prioritizing Your Acquisitions: Establishing clear goals also helps you make smart choices about which coins to add to your collection. This way, every new addition is a step toward fulfilling your overall vision, enhancing both the value and the coherence of your collection. It's a strategic approach that not only saves you money but also prevents you from making impulsive purchases that don't align with your goals (*Four Easy Steps to Becoming a Coin Collector*, 2015).

Staying Focused on Your Objectives: Coin collecting offers an abundance of choices, which can be both exciting and overwhelming. Setting goals acts as a compass, keeping you focused on what you aim to achieve. This focus is crucial for building a collection that not only mirrors your personal interests and passions but also has the potential to be valuable and significant within the numismatic community.

Understanding Your Motivation

In Chapter One, we explored the various motivations behind why people are drawn to coin collecting. From the historical significance and artistic appreciation to the investment potential, relaxation and thrill of the hunt, and the importance of legacy building and family tradition, each collector has their unique reasons that fuel their passion for this hobby.

Reflecting on what we discussed in the last chapter and considering your own journey into coin collecting, here are some prompts to help you explore different facets of your motivations and interests:

- **Historical Connection:** What about the history encapsulated within coins fascinates you the most? Is it the story of civilizations, the economic implications, or the personal narratives that each coin might have witnessed?
- **Artistic Beauty:** How does the artistry of coins influence your appreciation for them? Do you find yourself drawn to the craftsmanship, the designs, or the materials used in minting?
- **Investment Value:** Are you intrigued by the potential financial gain from coin collecting? What does the thrill of finding an undervalued coin or realizing the appreciation of your collection mean to you?

- **Pleasure and Relaxation:** Does coin collecting offer you a sense of relaxation or satisfaction? How does the process of searching for, discovering, and organizing your coins contribute to your well-being?
- **Family Tradition and Legacy:** Is your interest in coin collecting rooted in family tradition or the desire to build a legacy? How important is it for you to pass on your collection and the stories behind it to future generations?

Identifying Your Collecting Focus

Whether you're drawn to the beauty of coin designs, the history they represent, or the challenge of finding rare and unusual pieces, coin collecting offers a diverse and rewarding hobby that can be tailored to fit any interest or budget (Bucki, 2023).

Date or Year Collections

Collecting coins issued within a specific year or range of years is both a personal and historical endeavor. Enthusiasts may seek coins from their birth year, a notable historical event, or when a coin series underwent a significant change. Notably, the 1909 Lincoln cents introduced the iconic Lincoln design, including the rare 1909-S V.D.B. Lincoln Wheat cent, celebrated for its rarity and historical significance. Collectors might also complete series like Peace dollars in uncirculated condition, blending historical appreciation with personal achievement.

Type or Design Collections

This strategy focuses on collecting coins based on their design, including various denominations or commemorative issues. In the United States, this might mean assembling a collection that spans the Shield Nickel, Liberty Head (V) Nickel, Buffalo Nickel, and Jefferson Nickel, demonstrating the evolution of nickel designs over time. The excitement for design diversity is evident, with collectors assembling collections that include both uncirculated Franklins and Roosevelts, drawn to their design and accessibility.

Mint or Mint Mark Collections

Coins produced at specific mints, identifiable by mint marks, are of particular interest. The Carson City mint ("CC" mint mark) coins are prized for their historical significance and rarity. A Carson City mint type set could feature the Liberty Seated Dime and the Morgan Dollar, reflecting the allure of specific mints and the pursuit of series incorporating sought-after mint marks.

Country or Region Collections

Gathering coins from certain countries or regions reflects the collector's heritage or travel experiences. Starting with accessible coins and gradually seeking rarer issues, collectors might compile coins from each country they've visited or focus on nations with rich numismatic traditions. The journey of collecting Canadian commemoratives, for example, ties personal heritage to the expansive numismatic landscape.

Theme or Topic Collections

Coins that depict animals, plants, buildings, or historical figures are sought for theme-based collections. Collectors enjoy the variety and significance of designs across different countries and eras. The thematic depth encourages collectors to explore specific motifs or stories, such as the detailed die marriages found in bust halves.

Variety or Error Collections

The anomalies in coin production, including double dies, off-center strikes, and planchet errors, intrigue certain collectors. These errors, creating unique coins, are coveted for their rarity and the tales of their unusual production. The community of collectors focusing on such divergences is passionate, showing the broader appeal of collecting coins marked by distinctive errors.

Grade or Condition Collections

Seeking coins of a specific grade or condition involves patience and potentially significant investment but can culminate in a highly valuable and aesthetically pleasing collection. The commitment is clear, as collectors discuss upgrading older circulated coins to brilliant uncirculated conditions, illustrating a dedication to enhancing the quality of their collections. A coin graded MS-70 represents the pinnacle of perfection in this scale, indicating a mint-state coin with no post-production imperfections visible under 5x magnification, thus making it highly sought after for its flawless condition.

Period Collections

Concentrating on coins from certain historical periods offers a tangible connection to history. Whether it's Roman Empire coins, medieval times, or any other era, collectors immerse in the history and artistry through numismatics. The focus on European coins from regions that ceased minting by 1800 exemplifies a deep appreciation for historical narratives through coin collecting.

Value or Rarity Collections

Chasing coins known for their high value or rarity poses unique challenges and rewards. These collections often signify considerable financial and historical value. The dedication to amassing significant collections is highlighted by the pursuit of specific rare varieties and the commitment to completing comprehensive variety sets.

SETTING SMART GOALS

SMART goals—Specific, Measurable, Achievable, Relevant, and Time-bound—provide a framework for setting clear and attainable objectives. This approach ensures that coin collectors set realistic targets, enhancing their experience and satisfaction. Whether you're a beginner or a seasoned collector, SMART goals help to focus efforts, streamline the collecting process, and ensure progress and achievement are clearly defined and attainable.

- **Specific:** Define what you aim to collect, such as completing a Lincoln Wheat Penny Date Collection or assembling a 20th Century Basic Collection. The more precise your goal, the easier it is to plan your collecting journey.

- **Measurable:** Establish criteria to measure progress. For example, acquiring all the quarters from the U.S. state and national landmarks series or obtaining specific coins within a budget under $100, as outlined in collections that can be assembled affordably.
- **Achievable:** Ensure your goals are within reach. Starting with coins found in pocket change or focusing on more common, less expensive coins can make your hobby both enjoyable and feasible.
- **Relevant:** Choose goals that are meaningful to you. Whether it's collecting coins from your birth year or focusing on specific historical periods, your collection should reflect your interests and passions.
- **Time-bound:** Set deadlines. Whether it's completing a collection within a year or obtaining a rare coin by saving up, having a timeline helps maintain focus and momentum.

Setting Your Own SMART Goals

Reflect on what aspects of coin collecting excite you the most and use the SMART framework to outline your goals. Remember, the journey of collecting is personal and should be tailored to what you find most fulfilling. Here are some examples:

- **Completing a Series:** You could assemble a complete collection of 3 cent nickels, both clad and silver. This goal is specific (clearly defined series), measurable (completion can be clearly identified), achievable (focused on a specific series within reach), relevant (significant personal interest), and time-bound (aiming to find the rarer pieces within a set timeframe).

- **Diverse Collecting Within a Theme:** Some collectors set out with no specific goal but find joy in acquiring coins from different mints and countries, aiming for something like a total weight of 1000 oz. This approach, while broader, still fits within the SMART framework, especially as the collector sets a clear, measurable target for the total weight of coins to be collected.
- **Investment Focused:** Perhaps you want to focus on silver and gold as a form of investment, and set a goal to cover all holdings through profits from selling parts of the collection. This goal is strategic, emphasizing the relevance and achievability of investing in precious metals while also being measurable and time-bound, with the intent of achieving self-sustainability. (*What Is Your Coin Collecting Goal?*, 2022)

Guide to Setting Your SMART Goals

- **Identify What Excites You:** Whether it's the artistic design of coins, their historical value, or the investment potential, pinpoint what aspect of coin collecting draws your interest the most.
- **Set a Specific Target:** Define exactly what you aim to achieve. Is it completing a series? Acquiring coins from a particular era or mint? Setting an investment goal?
- **Measure Your Progress:** Establish clear indicators of progress. If your goal is to complete a series, keep a checklist. For investment goals, monitor the market value and your collection's weight.
- **Ensure Goals Are Achievable:** Start with goals within your reach. Consider your budget, resources, and the

availability of coins. Break down larger goals into smaller, manageable steps.
- **Align With Your Interests:** Make sure your goals resonate with your passions within the hobby. Collecting should be enjoyable and fulfilling.
- **Timeframe:** Set deadlines. Whether it's completing a part of your collection by the year's end or achieving a certain investment milestone in five years, timelines provide motivation and structure.

TRACKING YOUR PROGRESS AND ADJUSTING GOALS

To enhance your coin collecting journey and ensure you meet your goals, it's vital to regularly track your progress and be willing to make necessary adjustments. Your interests may evolve, or you might encounter unexpected hurdles or opportunities. By being open to adjusting your goals and strategies, you ensure that your coin collecting journey remains enjoyable, rewarding, and aligned with your personal aspirations.

Stay Accountable: By setting clear goals for your coin collection—whether it's acquiring specific coins, reaching a particular number, or achieving a set value—and tracking these goals, you'll likely stay more committed. Regularly reviewing your progress keeps you motivated and reduces the temptation to stray from your objectives. Just as importantly, holding yourself accountable can help prevent procrastination, ensuring you remain active in your pursuit of new additions to your collection.

Measure Progress: Tracking allows you to see how much closer you've come to achieving your collection goals. This not only serves as a powerful motivator but also helps you appreciate the journey. By measuring your progress, you can also identify what steps you've taken and recognize any achievements, big or small. It's a way to see how each new coin or learned piece of numismatic knowledge contributes to your larger goal.

Identify Roadblocks: Regularly evaluating your progress helps pinpoint potential obstacles, such as budget constraints, difficulty finding specific coins, or even waning interest in a particular area of collecting. Recognizing these challenges early on provides an opportunity to address them head-on, whether that means reallocating resources, seeking advice from fellow collectors, or refocusing your collection goals to reignite your passion.

Make Adjustments: The coin collecting landscape is dynamic, with market values fluctuating and new discoveries continually being made. Tracking your goals and progress allows you to identify when adjustments might be necessary. For instance, if you find yourself consistently unable to acquire coins in a particular category due to their rarity or cost, it might be time to pivot to a more accessible or personally meaningful area of collecting.

CONSIDERING BUDGETARY CONSTRAINTS

Don't let the idea that coin collecting is expensive hold you back. You can start and grow a collection with any budget by looking for affordable options and managing your collection wisely.

Setting a Budget for Yourself

Establishing a budget is the first step to a disciplined approach to collecting. Determine an amount you're comfortable spending, considering both acquisitions and the necessary supplies for preserving your collection. This budgetary cap ensures that your passion for collecting remains a source of joy rather than financial stress.

Start With the Change in Your Pocket

Your journey into coin collecting can begin with something as simple as the change in your pocket. Everyday transactions might yield coins with historical or collectible value, which can serve as the seeds of an impressive collection over time.

Familiarize Yourself With Catalogs and Genuine Online Websites

Knowledge is power in the world of numismatics. Spend time exploring catalogs and reputable online resources to understand the market, identify coins of interest, and discern their fair market value. This research is instrumental in making informed decisions and spotting deals.

Search the Discount Bin at Your Local Coin Dealer

Local coin shops often have discount bins where you can find coins at lower prices. These bins can be treasure troves for collectors on a budget, offering the chance to add to your collection without straining your finances.

Make the Most of Coin Collecting Apps and Resources

Technology offers coin collectors powerful tools for managing their collections and staying informed about the market. Utilize coin collecting apps and online resources to track your collection, identify wish-list coins, and connect with the broader collecting community.

Affordable Coins for Beginner Collectors

For those starting out, certain coins offer both affordability and collectible appeal. For instance, Lincoln Wheat Pennies, Jefferson Nickels, and Roosevelt Dimes are excellent starting points, offering historical significance and a wide variety of designs without the hefty price tag of more rare specimens (*10 Coin Collections You Can Assemble for under $100*, 2021).

GATHERING THE ESSENTIAL TOOLS FOR COIN COLLECTING

- **Magnifying Glass:** For coin collectors, a magnifying glass is essential to inspect coins closely and identify any imperfections or counterfeit items. There are primarily two types available: handheld magnifiers, which are portable and convenient for quick inspections, and illuminated magnifying lamps that offer additional lighting to help see details more clearly, though they are larger and less portable. Handheld models offer the advantage of portability, but might not provide sufficient magnification for all needs. On the other hand, illuminated magnifiers offer enhanced visibility at the cost of reduced portability.
- **Lighting:** Proper lighting is crucial for clear visibility of coins and to avoid eye strain during detailed examinations. Options include LED desk lamps, which offer clear and energy-efficient lighting, and adjustable

lighting setups that allow for flexibility in light direction and intensity. While LED lamps are durable and environmentally friendly, they may not fully illuminate every aspect of the coin (Jones, 2023). Adjustable lighting setups provide customizable lighting solutions but may be more costly and complex to install.

- **Viewing Pad:** Viewing pads offer a protective surface to examine coins without risking scratches. Available in various sizes and materials, these pads allow collectors to select the best option for their needs. The ability to choose specific sizes and materials enables customization, though some options may require additional maintenance or attract dust.
- **Gloves:** Gloves protect coins from the harmful effects of oils, dirt, and moisture from hands. Choices include cotton gloves, which are breathable and comfortable, and nitrile gloves, which offer protection against chemicals. While cotton gloves are preferred for their comfort, they may absorb oils. Nitrile gloves are effective in protecting against oils and moisture but may not offer the same level of comfort.
- **Digital Scale:** Weighing coins is a critical step in verifying their authenticity and condition. Digital scales that offer precise measurements to tiny fractions of a gram are invaluable for accurate assessments. High-precision scales provide exact readings but may be more expensive, while more affordable scales might lack the precision needed to detect minor yet significant weight differences.
- **Caliper:** Calipers are tools used to measure the diameter and thickness of coins, assisting in the identification of counterfeits. Digital calipers offer precise measurements

and are user-friendly but require batteries. In contrast, traditional calipers are durable and do not need batteries but are less precise and have a steeper learning curve.

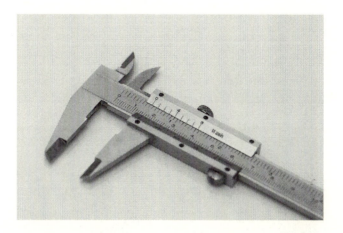

- **Coin Holder, Storage, and Display Solutions:** Keeping coins safe from damage is vital, and there are various options for storing and displaying them. Protective solutions like coin flips and capsules safeguard individual coins, while albums and trays help organize and display collections. Protective solutions ensure safety but may restrict visibility, whereas organizational tools like albums facilitate viewing but may offer less protection (Bucki, 2022).
- **Coin Reference Guide:** *The Official Red Book: A Guide Book of United States Coins* is an invaluable resource for identifying coins, including their history and current values. You may want to acquire other specialty publications depending on your particular collection and goals. Even in the digital age, guides are indispensable for collectors to accurately determine the worth of their coins.

SUMMARY

- **Embark on Your Expedition:** Think of yourself as an archaeologist on a quest to uncover the treasures of history and art through coins. Your journey is one of discovery, where setting clear goals is paramount. Whether your interest lies in ancient coins, modern designs, or specific historical periods, focusing your efforts based on your personal tastes will make your collection both meaningful and enjoyable.
- **Define Your Targets:** It's crucial to have specific aims for your collection. This clarity guides you through the vast expanse of numismatics, helping you prioritize which coins to pursue. This strategy not only keeps you focused but also ensures that each new addition is a valuable piece of the bigger picture you're assembling.
- **Explore Your Motivations:** Delve into what draws you to coin collecting. Is it the historical significance, the beauty of the designs, the potential for investment, or the thrill of the search? Understanding why you collect helps to sharpen your focus and makes the journey more fulfilling.
- **Choose Your Focus:** Your collection can take many forms. You might concentrate on coins from a specific year, type, mint, country, or even theme. This flexibility allows you to tailor your collecting to what interests you most, fitting your budget and what's available to you. It's all about finding what captivates you and pursuing it with passion.
- **Set SMART Goals and Gather Tools:** Adopting SMART goals (Specific, Measurable, Achievable, Relevant, Time-

bound) will help you navigate your collecting journey with purpose and clarity. Equally important is equipping yourself with the right tools—magnifying glasses, proper lighting, viewing pads, gloves, digital scales, calipers, and trusted reference guides. These tools are indispensable for inspecting, authenticating, and fully appreciating your coins.

CONCLUSION

This chapter provided you with the necessary knowledge to set clear, achievable goals and understand what motivates you in the world of numismatics. Equipped with a defined purpose and the right tools, you're prepared to enter the field. It's important to recognize that each coin in your collection represents more than just a piece of metal; it's a piece of history, a reflection of artistry, and an element of your personal legacy.

The next chapter will take you through a more detailed anatomy of coins, familiarize you with the specific language, and present the wide range of coins from various periods and locations. Utilizing technology, you'll be able to deepen your understanding of the distinctive features of coins, improving your ability to identify and categorize them. This knowledge will not only grow your appreciation for your collection but also refine your approach to selecting coins, ensuring that each new addition is a meaningful contribution to your collection, aligned with your goals and interests.

3

MASTERING COIN IDENTIFICATION

Coin collecting is heralded as one of the world's oldest and most captivating hobbies, boasting a rich heritage that dates back to kings and emperors who cherished the art and value of coins well before our modern era. This age-old tradition has been passed down through the ages, evolving into a vibrant and diverse pastime that appeals to enthusiasts from various backgrounds.

As noted in Chapter One, prominent historical figures such as Thomas Jefferson, John Quincy Adams, and esteemed artists like Goethe and Winckelmann, all shared a passion for coin collecting—a testament to its widespread appeal across different strata of society.

Adam Eckfeldt played a pivotal role in the early days of the U.S. Mint. Appointed as the second chief coiner in 1814, Eckfeldt's contributions were instrumental in the development of early American coinage. He established the Mint Cabinet, now part of the National Numismatic Collection, which was crucial in preserving a key selection of American coins and served as the foundation for numismatic study and collection in the United States.

Josiah K. Lilly Jr., an heir to the Eli Lilly pharmaceutical empire, channeled his considerable resources into creating one of the most extensive private coin collections in the world. His collection included rare gold coins from across the globe, showcasing not only the diversity of coinage but also the intricate artistry of minting. Today, his legacy endures at the Smithsonian Institution, where his collection continues to inspire and captivate coin enthusiasts.

King Farouk I of Egypt was known for his extravagant lifestyle and his equally impressive coin collection, which included some of the rarest and most valuable coins in the world. His collection was so extensive that after his abdication in 1952, the coins were auctioned in what is still considered one of the greatest coin sales of the twentieth century. Farouk's collecting activities highlighted how coin collecting could be a symbol of status and passion, providing a thrilling pursuit for both the collector and the spectator.

As you read this chapter on the parts and terms of coins, let the legacies of Eckfeldt, Lilly, and Farouk inspire your own collecting journey. With every coin you add to your collection, you engage in a narrative that links you to collectors across history, each piece a testament to the enduring beauty and legacy of coin collecting.

EXPLORING COIN ANATOMY AND TERMINOLOGY

Understanding the anatomy of a coin is important for anyone interested in coin collecting, grading, or evaluating coins. Each component of a coin's anatomy has distinct characteristics that can help identify, assess its condition, and understand its historical context. Each element also offers insights into the coin's history, design choices, and the technological capabilities of the mint that produced it.

Obverse

The obverse is considered the "front" side of the coin, typically featuring a portrait or the main design. This side is often referred to as the "heads" side, displaying images of monarchs, presidents, or allegorical figures to represent the issuing authority (Headley, 2021).

Reverse

The reverse, or "back" side of the coin, often referred to as the "tails" side, usually showcases a design or emblem representing the issuing nation's culture, history, or values. This side complements the obverse by offering additional space for artistic and symbolic expressions (*Reverse Side of a Coin*, n.d.). For example, the Canadian Loonie features a Loon on the reverse side, symbolizing tranquility and the natural beauty of Canada. This imagery reflects the nation's appreciation for its wildlife and environmental heritage.

Edge

The edge is the "third side" of a coin, running around its entire circumference. It can be plain, reeded, lettered, or decorated with various designs for security and aesthetic purposes (Headley,

2022). Edges are integral to preventing counterfeiting and clipping, ensuring the metal content's integrity.

- **Plain edges** are smooth and lack any inscription or design.
- **Reeded or milled edges** have grooves or ridges around the circumference, often used for added security.
- **Lettered edges** contain inscriptions or lettering, which can include mottos or other information relevant to the coin's theme.
- **Security edges** feature specific patterns or symbols designed to enhance anti-counterfeiting measures.
- **Decorated edges** may have intricate designs or textures, often used on commemorative or special-issue coins.
- **Grooved edges** are similar to reeded edges but with deeper, more pronounced grooves, providing a distinctive tactile feel.

Rim

The rim is the raised border on both the obverse and reverse sides of a coin, designed to protect the coin's design from wear (Headley, 2022). It frames the coin, giving it a finished look and helping to maintain its structural integrity during circulation.

Inscription

Inscriptions or legends on a coin include text such as the issuing country, denomination, year of minting, and other relevant details or mottos (*The Anatomy of a Coin Explained*, 2022). These elements are crucial for identifying and contextualizing the coin.

Mint Mark

A small letter or symbol indicating where the coin was minted. Mint marks provide insight into the coin's origin and can affect its rarity and value (*Mint Marks*, n.d.). The mint mark appears on the obverse ("heads") side of a coin, just below the date.

Field

The field is the flat, background area of the coin's surface, surrounding the raised design elements (relief). It often plays a role in the coin's aesthetic appeal and condition assessment (*The Anatomy of a Coin*, 2018).

Relief

The raised part of a coin's design, including images and text. The relief contrasts against the field, making the design stand out. The condition of the relief is a key factor in grading a coin (*The Anatomy of a Coin*, 2018).

Incuse

Designs or elements impressed into the surface of the coin, creating a recessed effect. Incuse designs are less common and can provide a unique aesthetic and tactile experience (McMorrow-Hernandez, 2021).

UNDERSTANDING DIFFERENT TYPES OF COINS

The number of different kinds of coins in circulation, commemorative issues, and investment categories is vast and varied, spanning numerous countries, historical periods, and purposes. Coins intended for collection rather than everyday currency are known as numismatic coins. Numismatic coins are valued for their rarity, historical significance, and collectibility, and may include both circulated and uncirculated coins. Unlike uncirculated coins, which are prized for their mint condition, numismatic coins can also be sought after for their historical context and unique characteristics. Here's an overview of some other types you might find in collections:

Circulated Coins

Circulated coins are those that have been issued by the mint and have seen use in daily transactions. These coins can range from current currency to older issues that have been retired from circulation and reflect the era in which they were used.

- **Lincoln Wheat Penny (1909–1958):** Recognizable by the two wheat ears on the reverse side, this coin reflects the era in which it was used. It's a common starting point for collectors due to its historical significance (*Circulating Coins*, n.d.).
- **George Washington Quarter (1932–1998):** This series includes the Bicentennial Quarter (1975–1976) and the 50 State Quarters Program (1999–2008), reflecting significant moments in U.S. history.

- **Buffalo Nickel (1913–1938):** Known for its distinct depiction of an American bison, this coin is a favorite among collectors due to its iconic design and the era of American history it represents.
- **Mercury Dime (1916–1945):** Featuring Liberty with a winged cap, this design is often mistaken for Mercury, hence its name. It's highly sought for its artistic merit.
- **Roosevelt Dime (1946–Present):** Introduced shortly after President Roosevelt's death to honor his founding of the March of Dimes, this coin continues to circulate and serves as a reminder of his legacy.
- **Kennedy Half Dollar (1964–Present):** Issued shortly after JFK's assassination, it was quickly adopted by the public for its commemorative value and is still in circulation today.

- **Susan B. Anthony Dollar (1979–1981, 1999):** This coin marked a shift in the design of US coinage by featuring a non-fictional female figure, representing the women's suffrage movement.

Commemorative Coins

Commemorative coins are issued to honor significant events, individuals, or anniversaries. These coins are usually produced in limited quantities and are not intended for general circulation. For example, the U.S. Mint has issued commemorative coins for events like the bicentennial of the United States (*Circulating Coins*, n.d.). These coins often have unique designs reflecting the event or individual they commemorate, making them highly sought after by collectors.

- **Lincoln Bicentennial One Cent Program (2009):** Celebrates the 200th anniversary of President Abraham

Lincoln's birth. Each design represents a different aspect of Lincoln's life.

- **America the Beautiful Quarters® Program (2010–2021):** Features national parks and sites from each state, district, and territory of the U.S., highlighting the beauty and diversity of the country.
- **Civil Rights Act of 1964 Silver Dollar (2014):** Issued to commemorate the 50th anniversary of the signing of the Civil Rights Act, this coin features iconic images associated with the civil rights movement.
- **Lewis and Clark Exposition Gold Dollar (1904–1905):** Minted to commemorate the centennial of the Lewis and Clark Expedition, featuring portraits of the explorers.
- **Apollo 11 50th Anniversary Coins (2019):** Celebrate the first manned moon landing with designs that include depictions of an astronaut and the lunar surface.
- **Star-Spangled Banner Commemorative Coin (2012):** Features elements of the War of 1812 and the famous flag that inspired the national anthem.
- **Jamestown 400th Anniversary Silver Dollar (2007):** Honors the first permanent English settlement in America, featuring images of a Native American, a European, and an African, symbolizing the diverse cultures involved.

Bullion Coins

Bullion coins are precious metal coins intended for investors. They are valued by the weight of the precious metal they contain, such as gold, silver, or platinum. Bullion coins' values fluctuate with the market price of the metal.

- **American Eagle Gold Coin:** Offered in various weights, these coins are a cornerstone of precious metal investing, with their value tied to the market price of the metal (*What Are Bullion Coins?*, 2021).

- **Canadian Maple Leaf:** Available in gold, silver, and platinum, these coins are known for their purity and are sought after for both investment and collection.
- **Australian Kangaroo Gold Coin:** Known for its annually changing design of a kangaroo, Australia's most iconic animal.
- **Austrian Philharmonic:** Available in gold, silver, and platinum, these coins are popular due to their elegant design featuring musical instruments.
- **Chinese Panda:** Unique in that its design changes every year, adding to its appeal among collectors and investors alike.
- **South African Krugerrand:** One of the first gold bullion coins available for private investment, its design features the Springbok antelope.
- **Mexican Libertad:** Offers both gold and silver variants and is recognized for its depiction of the iconic Angel of Independence.

Ancient Coins

Ancient coins offer a glimpse into the monetary systems of past civilizations, such as the Roman Empire, Greek city-states, and ancient China. These coins not only served as currency but also as a means for rulers to disseminate propaganda and messages to the populace.

- **Denarius:** A silver coin used in Ancient Rome, serving not only as currency but also as a tool for rulers to communicate with their subjects (*The Brief History of World Coins*, 2017).

- **8 Reales ("Piece of Eight"):** A Spanish coin that played a crucial role in the global trade system, known for its silver content and historical significance.
- **Tetradrachm (Ancient Greece):** Widely used during the height of Greek civilization, often bearing the face of Athena and the owl of wisdom.
- **Solidus (Byzantine Empire):** A gold coin used during the Byzantine Empire's peak, known for its high purity and weight consistency.
- **Stater (Ancient Lydia):** One of the earliest coins made from electrum, a natural occurring alloy of gold and silver.
- **Aureus (Ancient Rome):** A high-value gold coin used throughout the Roman Empire, prized for its detailed portraiture of emperors.
- **Shekel of Tyre (Phoenicia):** Famous for its depiction of Melqart, a god equated with Hercules, and widely known as the "thirty pieces of silver" paid to Judas.

World Coins

World coins refer to coins from countries other than one's own. Collecting world coins can offer insights into the culture, history, and art of different nations. For instance, the Canadian Maple Leaf and the British Sovereign are popular among collectors for their designs and gold content (*The Brief History of World Coins*, 2017). Collecting world coins is a way to travel the globe through numismatics.

- **Canadian Maple Leaf:** As mentioned, it's a popular choice for collectors interested in foreign bullion coins.

- **Yap Stones:** Large stone discs used as currency on the island of Yap, showcasing the diversity of forms that money can take around the world.
- **British Sovereign:** Renowned for its depiction of St. George slaying the dragon, valued both for collection and investment.
- **French Franc:** Once the cornerstone of the French economy, these coins offer a glimpse into France's rich political and cultural history.
- **Russian Ruble:** Features iconic Russian imagery, providing insights into the country's vast history and changes in political regimes.
- **Indian Rupee:** Displays India's historical and cultural richness through its series of coins depicting various emblems and figures.
- **Brazilian Real:** Offers diverse designs depicting Brazil's wildlife and cultural heritage, appealing to collectors interested in South America.

Proof Coins

Proof coins are the highest quality coins produced by the mint, featuring a mirror-like finish. They are made using specially treated blanks and dies, resulting in coins with sharp details and a shiny background. Proof coins are usually sold in sets and come with a Certificate of Authenticity from the mint (Headley, 2022b).

- **Modern Proof Coins:** Characterized by their mirror-like fields and frosted devices, often sold in sets with a Certificate of Authenticity from the mint.
- **Cameo Proof Coins:** These exhibit a distinct contrast between the frosted design elements and the mirrored

background, achieved through specialized minting processes.

Error Coins

Error coins are mint mistakes that escape into circulation. These can include off-center strikes, double dies, and blank planchets. Collectors prize error coins for their rarity and uniqueness, making them a fascinating category of coin collecting. An example is a double die penny, where the coin's design appears doubled (Headley, 2022b).

Uncirculated Coins

Uncirculated coins are those that have never been used in transactions and retain their original mint condition. They often have a higher quality finish than circulating coins but are not as finely made as proof coins (*What Are Bullion Coins?*, 2021). Collectors seek uncirculated coins for their pristine condition and potential for appreciation in value.

- **American Innovation™ $1 Coin Program:** This series features $1 coins in pristine condition, never used for transactions, highlighting American ingenuity.
- **Native American $1 Coin Program:** Celebrates the contributions of Native Americans with coins that are kept in uncirculated condition for collectors.
- **Presidential $1 Coin Program (2007–2016):** This series features coins with the likenesses of each U.S. President in the order that they served. The uncirculated versions are prized for their excellent finish and historical significance.

- **50 State Quarters Program (1999–2008):** This innovative program produced quarters representing each of the 50 states with unique designs that celebrated their history and heritage. Uncirculated versions of these quarters are particularly sought after due to their mint condition and the wide variety of designs.

UTILIZING TECHNOLOGY FOR COIN IDENTIFICATION

Utilizing technology in the realm of coin collecting has revolutionized the way collectors identify, grade, and value their coins. With advancements in artificial intelligence (AI), machine learning, and image recognition technology, numerous applications and online resources have emerged, providing collectors with powerful tools at their fingertips.

AI in Coin Identification

Apps like CoinSnap and Coinoscope leverage AI-driven image recognition technology to accurately identify coins. CoinSnap, for example, allows users to take a picture of a coin, which the app then matches to its database, providing details such as the coin's name, country of origin, year of issue, and an estimated value. This tool not only identifies the coin but also grades it, giving collectors a preliminary idea of the coin's condition without the need for immediate professional evaluation.

Online Resources

- **CoinSnap:** For quick identification and grading based on image recognition, CoinSnap is a robust app with a

significant user base and high accuracy for common coins.
- **Coinoscope:** Offers similar functionality to CoinSnap, with the added benefit of being directly linked to extensive online databases for further research.
- **Numiis:** An excellent online resource for those seeking detailed information about their coins, including year, mint, and accurate market value, based on advanced AI algorithms.
- **PCGS CoinFacts App:** Recommended for collectors who seek the backing of the Professional Coin Grading Service, offering detailed coin information and grading standards.

SUMMARY

- **Coin Anatomy and Terminology:** A thorough understanding of coin anatomy is crucial for collectors. The chapter breaks down essential components like the obverse (front), reverse (back), edge, rim, inscriptions, mint mark, field, relief, and incuse. Each element plays a significant role in a coin's identification, value, and historical context, underscoring the importance of knowledge in appreciating and collecting coins.
- **Diverse Types of Coins:** The chapter categorizes coins into circulated, commemorative, bullion, ancient, world, proof, error, and uncirculated coins, each with unique characteristics and significance. This diversity offers collectors a wide range of interests and focuses within the hobby, from historical coins like the Denarius to

investment-focused bullion coins and the high-quality finishes of proof coins.

- **Technological Advancements in Coin Collecting:** Advancements in technology, particularly AI and image recognition, have transformed how collectors identify, grade, and value their coins. Applications like CoinSnap and Coinoscope provide accessible tools for quick identification and preliminary grading, marking a significant evolution in the hobby. These tools democratize access to information, making the hobby more accessible to a broader audience.

CONCLUSION

Coin collecting combines the appreciation of beauty, history, and value into a single, engaging hobby. From the stories of historical figures like Thomas Jefferson and John Quincy Adams to modern enthusiasts like Josiah K. Lilly Jr. and King Farouk I, it transcends generations and cultures.

This chapter covered a detailed anatomy of coins, breaking down their various parts and terms, from the obverse and reverse to the intricacies of the rim, inscriptions, and mint marks. We also explored the vast diversity of coins, from circulated and commemorative coins to bullion, ancient, and proof coins, each category offering its own unique allure and challenges. Technology's role in coin collecting has been transformative, with AI and online resources like CoinSnap and Coinoscope revolutionizing how collectors identify, grade, and value their treasures. These advancements have made the hobby more accessible and informative, opening up new possibilities for collectors of all levels.

As we anticipate the next chapter, *Understanding the Minting Process*, we prepare to uncover the intricate processes behind coin creation, offering an inside look at the journey from design to circulation. This blend of craftsmanship and technological innovation brings coins to life, and we'll explore how these tiny artifacts are then introduced and distributed in the market.

4

UNDERSTANDING THE MINTING PROCESS

Step into the U.S. Mint, a place where advanced technology and traditional craftsmanship converge in the intricate art of coin making. The room buzzes with the rhythmic sound of machinery and the metallic clinks of coins being processed. Each corner of the facility hums with activity, but the die-making station stands out for its precise and meticulous operations.

Here, a seasoned engraver focuses intently on a new task—creating the die for a commemorative coin. This coin, destined to celebrate a historic national event, requires exceptional attention to detail. The engraver uses high-precision tools to carve out minute details into a small steel disc, which will serve as the master die. Every line and curve is expertly etched, from the subtle features of the figure depicted to the crisp clarity of the inscriptions around the coin's edge.

As the craftsman works, the importance of each stroke is palpable. The die will soon press thousands of coins, each carrying this artwork into pockets and collections across the country. This is more than manufacturing; it's a form of legacy creation, where artistry is stamped into metal and circulated through the hands of the nation. Watching the process, one gains a deeper appreciation for the coins that pass through our lives, each bearing silent testimony to the blend of technology and human skill that created them.

Have you ever pondered the sheer ingenuity and artistry required to transform a simple piece of metal into a work of art that you can hold in your hand? What does it take to etch history onto the surface of a coin, ensuring each design not only commemorates a significant event but also withstands the test of time? As you step into the world of die-making at the U.S. Mint, consider the depth of precision and creativity invested in each coin. How does this blend of old-world craftsmanship and modern technology influence the quality and aesthetics of the coins you encounter every day? We invite you to wade deeper into the art and science of coin production, to appreciate the meticulous craftsmanship behind each curve and contour, and to explore how each coin is a tiny monument to the era it represents.

WHAT IS A MINT?

A mint is an institution authorized by a country's government to manufacture coins that serve as legal tender, alongside other numismatic items such as collector coins and medals. These facilities play a crucial role in the economy by ensuring the supply of currency and also contribute to national heritage through the creation of commemoratives and bullion products.

Government Mints: Government or sovereign mints produce coins that are recognized as legal tender within the country. These mints adhere to strict standards set by the government, ensuring the coins' weight, purity, and face value. Sovereign mints often issue annual coin series that are eagerly anticipated by collectors and investors worldwide for their design, purity, and the government guarantee of their specifications. The United States Mint, for example, is a notable government mint, producing billions of coins each year for circulation, alongside precious metal bullion and collectible coins. It operates under the U.S. Department of the Treasury and is renowned for its contribution to the country's monetary system since 1792 (*What Is a Mint?*, 2021).

Private Mints: In contrast, private mints operate independently of government mandates and do not produce legal tender. Instead, they focus on bullion products, collectible coins, and medals, often for investors and collectors. These mints are known for their innovative designs and can produce items with a wider variety of metals and artistic elements, not bound by the requirements for circulation coins. Private mints have the flexibility to create coins and bullion that reflect cultural themes, historic events, or even popular collectible series, catering to a niche market of collectors and precious metal investors (*Mints of the World*, n.d.).

Evolution of Minting Throughout History

The minting process has undergone remarkable transformations over centuries, evolving from rudimentary methods to sophisticated, technology-driven processes. This journey from ancient molds to electric presses not only reflects the technological progress of humanity but also highlights how the minting process has adapted to meet the economic, cultural, and security needs of societies throughout history (*Coin Minting Technology throughout the Ages*, 2019).

We know that coinage is believed to have originated in the 7th century BCE in Lydia, modern-day Turkey. The concept quickly spread across the Mediterranean and into Europe and Asia, with coins initially being cast in molds. This method was eventually supplemented and then replaced by hammering, where a die with a design was stamped onto a metal blank with a hammer, a labor-intensive process requiring significant skill.

The advent of the screw press in the 16th century marked a significant advance in minting technology. This allowed for more consistent pressure during the striking process, enabling the simultaneous creation of both sides of a coin and enhancing the detail and uniformity of the designs. The era also saw the introduction of edge lettering and milling as anti-counterfeiting measures, significantly improving the security of coins.

The industrial and technological advancements of the 18th and 19th centuries brought steam-powered and later electric presses, revolutionizing coin production by significantly increasing output and efficiency. Modern minting processes involve highly automated systems that can produce millions of coins each day, with precision and designs that ancient minters could hardly have imagined. Today's mints also focus on security features to prevent counterfeiting, incorporating complex designs and materials into coins.

Renowned and Historic Mints

- **The United States Mint:** Known for its extensive security features and self-sustaining model, the U.S.

Mint is responsible for producing circulating coins, precious metals, collectible coins, and national medals for America.

- **The Royal Mint (UK):** With over 1,100 years of history, The Royal Mint is a storied institution responsible for producing the United Kingdom's currency, collector coins, and precious metals.

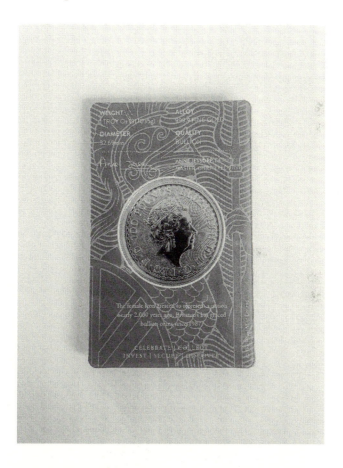

- **The Royal Canadian Mint:** Famous for its Gold and Silver Maple Leaf bullion coins, the Royal Canadian Mint produces all of Canada's circulation coins and offers refinery services.

- **The Perth Mint (Australia):** Australia's largest precious metals organization, known for its unique designs featuring Australian wildlife.
- **PAMP Suisse (Switzerland):** A pioneer in artistic bullion products, PAMP Suisse is renowned for its high-quality craftsmanship and the iconic "Lady Fortuna" design.
- **Monnaie de Paris (France):** As the world's oldest continuously operating mint, it has been producing coins and medals since AD 864, showcasing a rich history and a legacy of craftsmanship.

THE PROCESS OF COIN DESIGN

The design and production of coins involve a meticulous and collaborative process that integrates the talents of various professionals including artists, engravers, mint officials, and government authorities. This collective effort ensures that the coins not only serve as legal tender but also as artifacts of artistic expression and historical significance.

Overview of the Coin Design Process

The journey of a coin begins with the conceptualization of its design, which is often governed by legislation specifying themes or commemorations. Artists, both in-house at mints and external contributors through programs like the Artistic Infusion Program, submit design proposals. These designs undergo a rigorous review process involving multiple stakeholders including the Citizens Coinage Advisory Committee and the U.S. Commission of Fine Arts, ensuring that each design meets legal, artistic, and thematic criteria. Following approval by the Secretary of the

Treasury, the chosen design is transformed from a two-dimensional sketch into a three-dimensional model by skilled engravers. This model is then digitized to create the tools necessary for coin production. The final approval comes only after a successful test strike, ensuring the coin's design is suitable for mass production (*U.S. Mint Artistic Sculpting Process*, 2021; McVicker, 2022).

Notable Coin Artists and Engravers

The artistic heritage of coin design has been shaped by numerous talented individuals. Noteworthy among them are:

- **George T. Morgan:** Serving as the Chief Engraver at the United States Mint, Morgan is renowned for the Morgan Dollar, a design beloved by collectors for its aesthetic and historic value. His work is a testament to the intricate art of coin design that blends artistic vision with technical precision.
- **James Earle Fraser:** Known for the iconic Buffalo Nickel, Fraser's contributions reflect his expertise in sculpture and design, capturing the American spirit in coinage that remains popular among collectors.
- **Augustus Saint-Gaudens:** Commissioned by President Theodore Roosevelt, Saint-Gaudens redefined American gold coinage with his elegant designs, including the famous Double Eagle, which is celebrated as one of the most beautiful coins ever produced.
- **Victor David Brenner:** Best known for his design of the Lincoln cent, which was first issued in 1909 to commemorate the centennial of Abraham Lincoln's birth. Brenner's portrayal of Lincoln has become one of

the most recognized images in the United States, continuously in circulation for over a century.

- **Adolph A. Weinman:** Celebrated for designing the Mercury Dime and the Walking Liberty Half Dollar, Weinman's works are prized for their dynamic and lifelike imagery that epitomizes the freedom and progress of the early 20th century. His designs have influenced various modern coinages, including the American Silver Eagle, which revives his Walking Liberty.
- **John R. Sinnock:** As the eighth Chief Engraver of the United States Mint, Sinnock brought to life the Roosevelt Dime and the Franklin Half Dollar. His contributions are particularly noted for their clarity and the strength of their portraiture, which have helped make these coins staples in American commerce and collecting.
- **Elizabeth Jones:** Serving as the Chief Engraver from 1981 to 1991, Jones was the first woman to hold this position. She is known for her contributions to modern commemorative coins and medals, emphasizing bold and inspiring designs that have captured significant historical moments and figures.

THE PROCESS OF US COIN PRODUCTION

Understanding the intricacies involved in coin production enhances the appreciation of collectors for the craftsmanship behind each coin. The United States Mint's processes are meticulous and involve several stages to ensure quality and durability (*Coin Production*, 2024):

Step One: Blanking

The process begins with the creation of blanks, which are essentially flat metal discs cut from large coils of metal. This step is crucial as it sets the foundational shape for the final coins. The blanking press, a powerful machine, rapidly punches out these discs ensuring precision in diameter and thickness. This high-speed operation allows for the production of thousands of blanks per hour, preparing them for the subsequent stages of coin making. The quality of the blank is vital, as any imperfections could affect the final appearance and integrity of the coin.

Step Two: Annealing

Once the blanks are cut, they undergo annealing. This involves heating the metal discs to a specific temperature, which varies depending on the metal composition. The purpose of annealing is to soften the metal, making it more malleable and easier to imprint with detailed designs. This heating process must be carefully controlled to achieve the desired softness without compromising the metal's quality. After annealing, the metal becomes ductile, which is essential for absorbing the intricate details of the coin's design in the striking phase.

Step Three: Washing and Drying

After the annealing process, the blanks are washed to clean off any oxides or impurities that have formed on the surface during heating. This cleaning is typically done with a mild acidic solution that ensures the removal of all residues without damaging the metal. Following the wash, the blanks are thoroughly dried. This step is crucial to prevent any moisture from being trapped on the surface, which could lead to spotting or other defects during the striking process. Proper drying ensures that the blanks are pristine and ready for the next stage.

Step Four: Upsetting

In the upsetting stage, the previously flat edges of the blanks are carefully turned up to form a raised rim. This is done using an upsetting mill, which rolls the edges of the blanks to create a uniform rim. The raised rim not only enhances the structural integrity of the coin but also serves to protect the detailed design that will be imprinted on the coin's face and reverse sides. Additionally, this rim allows coins to stack neatly and be handled more easily by vending machines and counting devices.

Step Five: Striking

Striking is the transformative stage where the coin receives its final design. Each blank is placed between two dies that bear the negative of the coin's design. Under immense pressure, these dies come together to imprint the design onto the blank. This pressure must be precisely calibrated to ensure that the design is fully and clearly transferred, capturing even the finest details. This is where the softened, cleaned, and prepared blanks become recognizable coins, complete with images, inscriptions, and specific textures.

Step Six: Bagging and Packaging

The final stage involves inspecting, counting, and packaging the coins. Quality control is crucial here, as each coin is checked for defects and accuracy in design. Once approved, the coins are mechanically counted and bagged. Circulating coins are then distributed to Federal Reserve Banks, serving as the new currency for public use. Collectible coins, on the other hand, receive special handling, often being placed in protective casings with certificates of authenticity and packaged attractively to appeal to collectors and enthusiasts.

Coin Production Statistics and Data

The U.S. Mint's production varies significantly across different finishes. For standard use, circulation finish coins are produced in the highest volumes, ensuring enough coins for daily transactions. Proof finish coins, known for their mirror-like appearance and meticulous craftsmanship, are struck multiple times and primarily aimed at collectors. The uncirculated finish coins, while similar to regular circulation coins, are specially handled to prevent any marks or wear, also catering to collectors. Additionally, special mint sets are created with a distinct luster and limited production, offering something unique for serious collectors.

Facilities

The U.S. Mint operates multiple facilities, each with a specific focus. The Philadelphia facility is the workhorse, producing a wide array of coins including circulation types and various collector coins. Denver performs similarly, mainly producing circulation coins along with some collector items. The San Francisco facility is renowned for its proof coinage and other special collector products. West Point is primarily engaged in producing precious metal coins like gold, silver, and platinum American Eagles, as well as commemorative coins. The historical Carson City facility, now closed, was once known for its collectible value.

Denominations

Among denominations, pennies or cents are the most produced, usually tallying in the billions annually, made of zinc and coated with copper. Nickels, composed of a cupronickel alloy, are minted in the hundreds of millions. Dimes are also highly produced, often exceeding a billion pieces per year. Quarters see substantial production, especially with varying commemorative designs such as the America the Beautiful series. Half dollars and dollars, however, are minted in much smaller quantities, often directed more towards collectors than the general circulation.

In recent years, production data reflects shifts in demand and minting capacity. For example, in 2020, amidst the COVID-19 pandemic, the Mint increased its output by 23.7% due to a surge in demand for circulating coins (Bautista-González, 2023). This production included billions of coins, with pennies making up 47% of the Mint's total production in 2022, demonstrating the substantial scale of operations needed to meet the nation's needs for physical currency.

THE PROCESS OF COIN CIRCULATION

The circulation of coins through the economy is a complex process involving multiple stages and participants, ensuring that both new and existing coins are available for daily transactions. This circulation process not only ensures the availability of coins but also regulates the number of coins in the market, helping to maintain economic stability. (Meredith, 2020)

Initial Production and Forecasting

The U.S. Mint, responsible for coin production, collaborates closely with the Federal Reserve. The Mint does not distribute coins directly to the public but rather relies on the Federal Reserve Banks. These banks forecast demand for the next 12 months and place monthly orders with the Mint, influencing the production numbers for different denominations based on long-term demand and seasonal trends.

Manufacturing and Distribution

Once the production numbers are set, the Mint manufactures the coins, primarily at the facilities in Philadelphia and Denver. The coins are then securely transported via armored cars to the Federal Reserve Banks' 28 branch offices and over 100 private sector coin terminals. These terminals, operated by armored carriers contracted by the Federal Reserve, play a critical role in distributing coins.

Bank Distribution

Federal Reserve Banks distribute coins to depository institutions such as banks and credit unions. These institutions place their coin orders based on their needs, and the armored carriers transport the coins from the terminals to these institutions. The coins are then ready to enter general circulation.

Circulation Among Public and Businesses

The depository institutions distribute coins to businesses and individuals, facilitating their entry into everyday commerce.

These coins cycle between banks, businesses, and consumers, with banks redistributing both new and old coins. They also manage the return of excess coins to the Federal Reserve for redistribution or removal from circulation if they are worn out.

Out of Circulation

Not all coins remain in active circulation. Individuals often store coins in jars, piggy banks, or even collectors' vaults, temporarily reducing the number of coins in active circulation. These coins re-enter the cycle when spent or deposited at banks or coin exchange kiosks.

Importance in the Economy

This circulation process not only ensures the availability of coins for transactions but also regulates the number of coins in the market, helping to maintain economic stability. The Federal Reserve's role in forecasting and ordering facilitates precise control over coin distribution, which is essential for meeting the public's needs during different economic periods. Understanding this process highlights the logistical challenges and complexities involved in maintaining a functional currency system.

SUMMARY

- **Minting Institutions and Types:** A mint is a facility authorized by a government to produce coins used as legal tender, along with other numismatic items. There are both government mints, such as the United States Mint, which produce legal tender following strict national standards, and private mints, which create collectible and bullion products often focused on artistic and innovative designs.

- **Evolution of Minting Technology:** The methods and technologies for minting coins have evolved significantly over centuries—from ancient hand-hammering techniques to modern, high-speed, automated presses. This evolution reflects advancements in technology and the growing need for security features to prevent counterfeiting.
- **The Coin Design Process:** The design and production of coins involve a detailed and collaborative process that begins with a concept and undergoes several reviews and revisions before a final design is approved. This process ensures that the coins are not only functional as currency but also represent artistic and historical values.
- **Coin Production Steps:** The production of coins involves several key steps: blanking, annealing, washing and drying, upsetting, striking, and finally, bagging and packaging. Each step is crucial in ensuring the quality, durability, and security of the coins, demonstrating the intricate craftsmanship involved.
- **Coin Circulation:** The circulation of coins is a complex system managed by the collaboration between the Mint and the Federal Reserve. This system ensures that both new and recirculated coins are available to meet economic demands. Coins move through various channels including banks, businesses, and the public, and can exit circulation temporarily when collected or stored.

CONCLUSION

This chapter, "What is a Mint?", wandered into the fascinating world of mints, the specialized institutions responsible for coin production. These entities not only ensure a steady supply of currency but also contribute significantly to national heritage through the creation of collectible and bullion coins.

Expect to explore strategies for identifying genuine coins, understanding the markers of authenticity, and learning about the safeguards against counterfeit operations. Whether you're a seasoned collector or new to the field, this upcoming chapter will enhance your ability to engage confidently and securely in the coin collecting community.

THE SILENT STORIES OF YOUR COINS

No story lives unless someone wants to listen.

— J.K. ROWLING

A coin passes through many hands in its lifetime. Even the coins that are in circulation right now, the ones you may have on your nightstand or in the pocket of your jeans, have stories to tell. They're stories you will never hear. Perhaps one of them was given to a young boy by his grandma to buy candy... Maybe it was given to a busy working mom as change and then dropped in the street, later picked up by a girl who kept it as her lucky coin for a month before accidentally leaving it on a park bench, where someone in need picked it up... Each coin in your home has a story to tell, a story beyond economic evolution and the broader picture of monetary history.

Your coin collection holds these stories too – small personal stories about the people whose hands each coin has passed through. For all the history you will learn through coin collecting, you will also acquire a wealth of history you will never know, the quiet stories hidden in each coin.

I think there's something very beautiful about this. The way that coin collecting honors the people who have touched each piece and keeps something of their story alive, even if no one will ever hear it. Stories live on because they're shared. History is understood because we collect and explore the past. It is all an act of sharing and preserving the past, and it's in the spirit of this that I'd like to ask for your help in sharing the beauty of coin collecting with the world.

By leaving a review of this book on Amazon, you'll help new readers find it and begin their own journey with coin collecting.

Just as coins are passed from hand to hand, your words will pass to others, guiding them toward this rich history and the huge rewards it offers. Books allow us to share information and keep histories alive; reviews help them to spread further.

Thank you so much for your support. Each coin holds more history than you will ever know, and your words hold more power than you might expect. You're a vital part of this story.

Scan the QR code below

5

SOURCING YOUR COINS WISELY

The "Eid Mar" coin, famously known for commemorating the assassination of Julius Caesar, is an ancient silver denarius struck by Brutus in 42 BC. The coin's obverse features the bust of Brutus, while the reverse shows two daggers flanking a liberty cap—an emblem symbolizing the freedom from Caesar's rule. The inscription "EID MAR" beneath the daggers marks the Ides of March, the date of Caesar's assassination.

Genuine "Eid Mar" coins are exceedingly rare, with only about 80 confirmed examples known to exist. These coins are highly prized not only for their historical significance but also for their connection to one of the most pivotal moments in Roman history. The first known specimens were found in Europe in the early 19th century, and since then, each discovery has been a significant event within the numismatic community.

One such coin was purportedly discovered at a small auction in southern France and quickly caught the attention of collectors worldwide due to its well-preserved condition and sharp details.

However, upon detailed examination by experts, including assessments of the coin's metal content and engraving style, questions arose about its authenticity. The coin's weight was marginally lighter than other authenticated "Eid Mar" coins, and its patina suggested chemical treatment to simulate age.

Let this be a lesson that thorough research and expert verification matters when acquiring rare coins, no matter how experienced you are. Collectors are reminded that provenance, precise physical analysis, and consultation with trusted experts are essential steps to ensure the authenticity of such rare finds. The upcoming chapter will explore practical tips and strategies for sourcing coins wisely, helping you make informed decisions and avoid the pitfalls of sophisticated forgeries.

IDENTIFYING SOURCES FOR COINS

In the fascinating world of coin collecting, it's not just the value of the coins that captivates enthusiasts but also the thrill of the hunt. Coin dealers, both in physical stores and online, serve as gatekeepers to this treasure trove, offering everything from common coins to rare gems. Notably, the oldest coin ever discovered (The Lydian lion) is from the 7th century BC, a testament to the long history and enduring allure of coin collecting. Whether you're at bustling coin shows, navigating online marketplaces, or exploring forums and community groups, each source offers unique opportunities to add to your collection. As we delve into the various avenues for acquiring coins, remember that each piece holds a story, waiting to be discovered and preserved.

Coin Dealers

Coin dealers are professionals who specialize in buying, selling, and trading coins. These dealers can be found in both physical stores and online platforms. Brick-and-mortar shops offer the advantage of direct interaction, allowing you to inspect coins physically before purchasing. Online retailers, however, provide access to a broader inventory and the convenience of shopping from home. Reputable dealers often belong to numismatic associations, which can be a sign of credibility (Spurrier, 2022).

Coin Shows and Expos

Coin shows and expos are events where collectors and dealers gather to display, sell, and purchase coins. These events range from small local gatherings to large international expos and provide a unique opportunity to meet other collectors and experts. Coin shows also often feature auctions, where rare and valuable coins are sold to the highest bidder (*Coin Shows and Auctions*, 2023).

Online Marketplaces

Websites like eBay and other auction platforms are popular places for collectors to find and purchase coins. These sites offer a vast selection of coins from around the world, allowing collectors to bid on items remotely. It's important to verify the seller's reputation and the authenticity of the coins when using online marketplaces (Spurrier, 2022).

Numismatic Forums and Communities

Online forums and social media groups dedicated to coin collecting are invaluable resources. These platforms allow enthusiasts to share information, sell, trade, and buy coins directly from each other. Participating in these communities can also provide insights and advice from more experienced collectors (Golino, n.d.).

Banks

Banks can sometimes be sources for obtaining rolls of coins or bags of currency. Collectors often purchase these to find older, discontinued, or commemorative coins that are no longer in circulation. It's a more hit-or-miss approach but can yield interesting finds.

Estate Sales and Auctions

Estate sales and auctions can be treasure troves for coin collectors. These events may feature collections from estates where the owners collected coins, often including rare and valuable pieces. Attending these sales provides a chance to acquire unique coins that aren't available elsewhere (*Coins at Estate Sales*, 2022).

FINDING TRUSTED SOURCES

When considering a purchase, especially in niche markets like collectible coins, the reputation and credibility of sellers, dealers, and platforms are all important factors. This is needed to ensure authenticity, fair pricing, and ethical dealings. Here are some steps and strategies to help you assess these factors effectively:

- **Research Experience and Expertise:** A dealer's longevity in the business often correlates with their knowledge and reliability. Engage them in conversation to ascertain their specialization and experience in the field.
- **Check Professional Affiliations:** Membership in recognized organizations such as the Professional Numismatists Guild (PNG) or the American Numismatic Association (ANA) is a strong indicator of a dealer's credibility. These affiliations suggest adherence to certain ethical standards and professional practices.
- **Verify Business Ratings and Customer Reviews:** Look up the dealer or platform on review sites and check their Better Business Bureau (BBB) ratings. A high BBB rating and positive customer testimonials reflect a business's fairness and ethical conduct.
- **Assess Transparency and Communication:** Transparent dealers will freely share information about the items, including provenance and pricing methodology. They should be willing to answer questions and provide detailed product descriptions.
- **Examine Return Policies and Guarantees:** A trustworthy dealer often offers clear, customer-friendly return policies. This is indicative of confidence in the quality of their goods and a focus on customer satisfaction.
- **Consult Peer and Community Feedback:** Engage with online forums and community groups to hear firsthand

accounts of experiences with the dealer. Peer reviews can provide unfiltered insights into a dealer's practices.
- **Evaluate Ethics and Professional Conduct:** Ethical dealers conduct thorough and fair assessments of items and are upfront about any product issues. They adhere to a code of ethics that prioritizes transparency and fairness (Davis, 2012; Mark, 2017; McMorrow-Hernandez, n.d.).

VERIFYING COIN AUTHENTICITY

How can you be sure that the coins you've found or invested in are the real deal? Use one or a combination of these examinations and services to verify the coins you have or are adding to your collection (*Coins Authenticity Verification*, n.d.; *How to Authenticate Coins in Your Coin Collection*, n.d.; *Using Authentication and Grading Services*, n.d.):

Touch Test

The touch test involves feeling the coin for any irregularities. Key aspects to feel include the smoothness of the coin, the edge, and how the different parts of a bimetallic coin fit together. Any irregularity such as a slippery or soapy feel, or imperfections on the edge, might indicate a counterfeit.

To effectively conduct the touch test:

- **Feel the Texture:** Run your fingers over both the surface and the edges of the coin. Authentic coins typically have a consistent and smooth texture.

- **Check the Edges:** Examine the edges for any roughness or irregular patterns that might suggest tampering or counterfeiting.
- **Assess the Fit:** In the case of bimetallic coins, make sure the two different metals are seamlessly joined. A gap or mismatch suggests counterfeiting.

Visual Test

Visually inspect the coin for color consistency, brightness, and any signs of wear. Coins should not be discolored as they are not covered with any foreign material post-minting. Additionally, details such as microtext and latent images should be checked using a magnifying tool.

To enhance the visual inspection of your coins:

- **Examine Color and Finish:** Look closely for any unnatural coloration or finishing that might be a result of artificial treatment.
- **Use Magnification:** Employ a magnifying glass or a jeweler's loupe to inspect small details like microtext or intricate designs, which counterfeiters often struggle to replicate perfectly.
- **Check for Wear Consistency:** Ensure the wear on the coin matches its age and circulation history. Overly new appearances on old coins can be a red flag.

Sound Test

A sound test can help differentiate genuine coins from fakes. Genuine coins will produce a distinct metallic "twang" when tapped, whereas counterfeit coins might emit a dull sound due to materials like glue used in their fabrication.

For conducting a sound test:

- **Tap the Coin:** Strike the coin gently against another coin or a hard surface and listen to the sound it produces. Genuine coins have a clear, resonant ring, while fakes might sound dull or muffled.
- **Repeat Comparisons:** Compare the sound with that of a coin known to be authentic of the same type.

Weight and Diameter

Weighing and measuring the diameter of a coin can help verify its authenticity. Genuine coins have specific weights and measurements. Any significant deviation could indicate that the coin is counterfeit.

To verify by weight and diameter:

- **Use Precise Scales:** Weigh the coin on a digital scale accurate to at least two decimal places.
- **Measure the Diameter:** Use a caliper to measure the diameter of the coin, checking against official specifications.

Ice Cube

This test is based on the thermal conductivity of metals. Genuine silver coins will melt the ice at a noticeably faster rate than other metals, due to the high thermal conductivity of silver.

Magnet Test

Some metals used in coins are non-magnetic. Testing coins with a magnet can help identify non-authentic coins made from inappropriate magnetic materials.

To utilize the magnet test:

- **Use a Strong Magnet:** Gently bring a strong magnet close to the coin. Coins made of non-magnetic metals like gold and silver should not be attracted to the magnet.
- **Observe the Reaction:** Any magnetic pull indicates the presence of iron or steel, which are not used in genuine coins of precious metals.

Grading and Authentication Services

To ensure the authenticity of coins, use third-party authentication services. Companies like the Professional Coin Grading Service (PCGS), Numismatic Guaranty Corporation (NGC), and others are well-regarded in the industry for providing reliable services. These services evaluate the genuineness and grade of the coins, offering peace of mind when buying or selling. Follow their submission guidelines to send your coins for authentication, which will help determine not only authenticity but also the coin's grade.

Comparison and Reference

For collectors and enthusiasts, comparing a suspect coin with one that is known to be genuine is crucial. Utilize reference materials such as coin catalogs or online databases like *Numiis*, which offer detailed information about different coins and their characteristics. This approach helps in identifying discrepancies that could indicate a counterfeit. Focus on distinctive elements that are difficult to replicate accurately, such as the exact dimensions, design details, and material composition.

PROTECTING YOURSELF

A comprehensive strategy to safeguard your investments requires a discerning eye for value, a caution against deceptive practices, and an understanding of authenticity.

Price Research

As a coin buyer, thorough price research is imperative. Familiarize yourself with different price guides for retail and wholesale prices, such as the *Red Book* for retail and the *Blue Book* for wholesale values. This distinction is crucial since the price is what you pay, but the value is what you can sell the coin for, which often differs significantly. Use multiple price guides and recent auction records to understand the current market trends and price ranges for the coins you are interested in.

Avoiding Red Flags

Be vigilant of red flags when purchasing coins. Bad reviews, lack of affiliation with numismatic organizations, short business history, or inadequate evaluation of coins' conditions are signs of potential fraud. Always verify the seller's credentials, and if a deal seems too good to be true, it probably is (Allcot, 2023).

Knowing the Types of Counterfeit Coins

Educate yourself on the different types of counterfeit coins—struck, cast, and altered coins. Learn the common attributes of counterfeits and use available resources to understand how to spot them. If you suspect a coin might be counterfeit, seek a second opinion from a trusted source or use professional authentication services.

- **Struck Counterfeits:** Struck counterfeit coins are produced by striking a planchet (blank coin) between two counterfeit dies within a coining press. The counterfeit dies may be created through several methods, such as hand-engraving, using a transfer engraving lathe, or more advanced techniques like spark erosion. This process mimics the legitimate minting process, making struck counterfeits some of the most deceptive, as they can replicate the coin's relief and texture quite accurately. The quality of struck counterfeits varies, with some being easily recognizable upon close inspection, while others may require expert analysis to identify.
- **Cast Counterfeits:** Cast counterfeits are made by pouring molten metal into a mold that has been created from a genuine coin. This method is generally cheaper and easier than striking, but it also tends to produce coins of lower quality. Cast coins can often be identified by their lack of sharp detail, seam lines from the casting process, or a bubbly surface due to trapped air during casting. These flaws occur because the casting process is less precise than striking, resulting in a coin that may have a correct overall shape but lacks the refined details of a genuine struck coin.

- **Altered Coins:** Altered coins are genuine coins that have been modified in an attempt to make them appear more valuable. Common alterations include adding or removing mintmarks, changing dates, or manipulating the coin's surface. For example, a less valuable 1909 penny might be altered to look like a 1909-S VDB penny, which is worth significantly more. Altered coins may also include "coin doctoring," where a coin is artificially toned or its surface is altered to mask wear or damage. (Bucki, 2022b)

Paying Safely Online

Use secure and verified online payment methods that offer protection against fraud, like credit cards and PayPal. They provide a degree of security and recourse if the transaction is disputed or if you encounter fraudulent activity (*Shopping and Paying Safely Online*, n.d.).

Return Policies

Prior to purchase, confirm the seller's return policy. Ensure you understand the terms and conditions for returns and refunds. For example, the U.S. Mint limits returns from customers who have a history of excessive returns, indicating the importance of knowing a seller's return policy in detail.

SUMMARY

- **Diverse Sources:** Coin collectors have multiple sources to acquire coins, including coin dealers, coin shows, online marketplaces, numismatic forums, and even banks. Each source offers unique benefits, such as physical inspection at brick-and-mortar stores, a wide variety at online retailers, and the community and expertise found at shows and forums.

- **Verification and Authenticity:** It is crucial to verify the authenticity of coins before purchasing. Techniques like the touch, visual, and sound tests, as well as checking weight and using magnets, are simple ways to ensure authenticity. For higher assurance, collectors can also use professional grading and authentication services.
- **Community and Research:** Engaging with the numismatic community through forums and social media groups can provide invaluable insights and resources for both novice and experienced collectors. Additionally, researching a dealer's reputation, checking their affiliations with professional organizations, and reading customer reviews are essential to ensure credible transactions.
- **Understanding Counterfeits:** Knowledge of different types of counterfeit coins, such as struck, cast, and altered coins, is essential for collectors to protect themselves from fraud. Recognizing the common characteristics of fakes helps in identifying and avoiding them.
- **Safe Practices:** When purchasing coins, especially online, using secure payment methods and understanding return policies are important for protecting one's investments. Collectors should always conduct thorough price research to understand current market values and be cautious of deals that seem too good to be true to avoid potential scams.

CONCLUSION

As we wrap up this chapter on finding reliable coin sources, remember that successful collecting relies on careful selection and verification. Whether buying from dealers, attending shows, or engaging in online communities, always confirm the authenticity of coins using methods like the touch, visual, and sound tests. Engaging with the coin collecting community and using professional services also ensures you get genuine, valuable pieces.

In the next chapter, we'll dive into coin grading, a crucial skill for every collector. You'll learn about grading standards, the leading grading services, and practical techniques to evaluate your coins accurately. This knowledge will not only increase your collection's value but also boost your confidence and expertise as a collector. Get ready to sharpen your skills in coin grading.

QUIZ

We are now at the midpoint of *Coin Collecting for Beginners*. Take this opportunity to reinforce and assess your knowledge of the material we've explored so far with this quiz. Good luck!

ADVANCED INSIGHTS INTO COIN COLLECTING

Multiple Choice Questions

1. What is numismatics?

    - A) The study of numbers
    - B) The study and collection of currency
    - C) The study of historical artifacts
    - D) The study of stamps

2. Which of the following is NOT a reason why people collect coins?

- A) Historical fascination
- B) Investment potential
- C) Artistic appreciation
- D) Celebrity endorsements

3. What feature on a coin's edge is meant to prevent counterfeiting?

- A) Inscription
- B) Milled edge
- C) Field
- D) Relief

4. Which type of coin is known for being produced to commemorate specific events or people?

- A) Circulated coins
- B) Commemorative coins
- C) Bullion coins
- D) Proof coins

5. Which mint is responsible for producing the United Kingdom's currency?

- A) The Royal Canadian Mint
- B) The Perth Mint
- C) The Royal Mint
- D) The United States Mint

6. What does a coin's "obverse" refer to?

- A) The front, or "heads" side
- B) The back, or "tails" side
- C) The edge
- D) The rim

7. Which country first introduced milled edges on coins as a counterfeiting deterrent?

- A) France
- B) Italy
- C) Spain
- D) England

8. Which term refers to the raised boundary on a coin that helps protect its design?

- A) Rim
- B) Edge
- C) Field
- D) Inscription

9. Who is allowed to issue commemorative coins?

- A) Private mints
- B) Government mints
- C) Both A and B
- D) Neither A nor B

10. Which of the following stages in coin production involves heating the coin blanks to soften them?

- A) Blanking
- B) Annealing
- C) Upsetting
- D) Striking

11. Which type of coin is specifically designed for investment purposes?

- A) Commemorative coins
- B) Circulating coins
- C) Bullion coins
- D) Numismatic coins

12. Which of the following is NOT a feature of a coin?

- A) Legend
- B) Crest
- C) Rim
- D) Relicf

13. Which country is known for producing the American Eagle Bullion coins?

- A) Canada
- B) Australia
- C) United Kingdom
- D) United States

14. What element on the coin's design is intended to stand out from the background?

- A) Field
- B) Relief
- C) Rim
- D) Edge

15. Which of the following coins features an animal on its reverse side?

- A) U.S. Penny
- B) Canadian Loonie
- C) British Pound
- D) Euro

16. What is the main purpose of the milled edge on a coin?

- A) Decorative
- B) Protection against wear
- C) Prevent counterfeiting
- D) Indication of denomination

17. Where is the mint mark typically located on a coin?

- A) On the rim
- B) Below the obverse image
- C) On the edge
- D) Next to the date

18. What were early coins made from in the kingdom of Lydia?

- A) Gold
- B) Silver
- C) Bronze
- D) Electum

19. In coin collecting, what does "MS-70" grade signify?

- A) A coin with minor wear
- B) A coin with moderate defects
- C) A perfect uncirculated coin
- D) A circulated coin with no visible flaws

20. What is the primary benefit of coin collecting?

- A) Financial gain
- B) Educational value
- C) Artistic appreciation
- D) All of the above

True/False Questions

1. Numismatics is solely the study of coins. (True/False)
2. Coins are typically made from a single metal. (True/False)
3. Private mints can produce legal tender. (True/False)
4. All coins have an inscription on the edge. (True/False)
5. Coin collecting can be a form of investment. (True/False)
6. The obverse side of a coin is also known as the "tails" side. (True/False)

7. The first coins were created in the Roman Empire. (True/False)
8. A proof coin is intended for everyday transactions. (True/False)
9. Coin grading is a process that evaluates a coin's physical condition. (True/False)
10. The Royal Mint produces the currency for the United States. (True/False)

Fill-in-the-Blank Questions

1. The oldest coins were made in the kingdom of _____.
2. Coins that are no longer used for transactions and retain their original mint condition are referred to as _____ coins.
3. _____ is a type of edge with grooves or ridges designed to enhance security.
4. Coins from the _____ mint are known for featuring Australian wildlife in their designs.
5. The raised border on a coin that helps protect its design is called the _____.
6. A coin without any marks of wear and tear is considered to be in _____ condition.
7. Coins made from gold and silver are known as _____ coins.
8. _____ coins are specially made to highlight artistic detail and rarity.
9. Coins intended for collection rather than everyday currency are known as _____ coins.
10. The process by which a metal blank is prepared for minting is called _____.

ANSWERS

Multiple Choice

1. B, 2. D, 3. B, 4. B, 5. C, 6. A, 7. D, 8. A, 9. B, 10. B, 11. C, 12. B, 13. D, 14. B, 15. B, 16. C, 17. B, 18. D, 19. C, 20. D

True/False

1. False, 2. False, 3. False, 4. False, 5. True, 6. False, 7. False, 8. False, 9. True, 10. False

Fill-in-the-Blank

1. Lydia, 2. uncirculated, 3. Reeded, 4. Perth, 5. rim, 6. mint, 7. bullion, 8. Commemorative, 9. numismatic, 10. blanking

GRADING SCALE FOR QUIZ

- **36-40 correct answers: Excellent (90-100%)**

  - Exceptional understanding of the material with high proficiency demonstrated.

- **32-35 correct answers: Very Good (80-89%)**

  - Strong grasp of the content with minor areas for improvement.

- **26-31 correct answers: Good (65-79%)**

  ○ Solid comprehension, though some concepts may need further review.

- **20-25 correct answers: Satisfactory (50-64%)**

  ○ Adequate understanding, but further study and review are necessary.

- **14-19 correct answers: Needs Improvement (35-49%)**

  ○ Partial understanding with significant gaps in knowledge.

- **0-13 correct answers: Unsatisfactory (0-34%)**

  ○ Poor understanding, substantial improvement and additional study required.

6

NAVIGATING COIN GRADING

How did you do on the quiz? Just as coins are graded based on their condition, rarity, and overall quality, your quiz results reflect your comprehension and mastery of the material presented in the first half of the book. Think of the quiz as a numismatic grading system for your knowledge—where each correct answer helps determine your overall "grade."

In this chapter, we'll dive deeper into the fascinating world of coin grading, unveiling how nuanced details can significantly alter a coin's value and appeal. You'll learn about the meticulous criteria used to assess coins, such as wear and tear, luster, and the precision of the strike. We'll explore different grading systems, including the well-known Sheldon Scale and the British grading method, each offering unique perspectives on evaluating a coin's condition. Additionally, we'll discuss the importance of professional grading services and how they add credibility and trust to coin transactions. This knowledge will not only enhance your ability to appraise the coins in your collection but also equip you with the skills needed to make educated decisions in your collecting journey.

IMPORTANCE OF COIN GRADING

Coin grading is a critical process that evaluates and assigns a grade to a coin based on its condition. This system determines a coin's market value, historical significance, and overall collectibility. Here's a breakdown of the importance of coin grading and how it all works.

Key Factors Influencing Coin Grading

- **Wear and Tear:** The amount of wear and damage a coin has undergone directly affects its grade.

- **Luster:** The original sheen a coin had when it was minted, which diminishes with handling and age.
- **Strike:** The quality of the coin's imprint process, which affects how well the coin's designs and inscriptions are executed.
- **Eye Appeal:** Subjective assessment of a coin's aesthetic appeal.
- **Preservation:** How well the coin has been preserved from environmental damage such as corrosion or tarnishing.

Importance of Coin Grading

- **Market Value:** Graded coins can command higher prices on the market. The higher the grade, the more valuable the coin generally is, as collectors are willing to pay premium for coins in better condition.
- **Authenticity and Trust:** Professional grading by reputable services like PCGS (Professional Coin Grading Service) or NGC (Numismatic Guaranty Corporation) assures collectors of the coin's authenticity and condition.
- **Historical Significance:** Grading helps assess the historical wear and preservation, providing insights into the coin's lifespan and use.
- **Collectibility:** Collectors often seek out higher-grade coins for their collections because they tend to be rarer and more visually appealing.

Higher Grades Command Higher Prices

Graded coins are sought after for their certified condition and quality. This certification reduces the risk of counterfeits and incorrectly assessed coins, making them a safer investment. Collectors and investors are more confident in purchasing coins that have a clear, unbiased grade, which enhances their market value (*Is It Important to Grade Your Coins?*, n.d.).

GRADING STANDARDS AND SYSTEMS

Numerical scales are used world-wide. The Sheldon Scale, predominantly used in the U.S., offers a detailed 70-point assessment where higher numbers reflect better preservation and quality, with a score of 70 indicating a perfect, pristine coin. In contrast, the British Grading System employs descriptive terms such as Fine, Very Fine, and Uncirculated, focusing more on the coin's general condition and emphasizing wear, design sharpness, and overall aesthetic appeal, rather than specific numerical ratings. The NGCX 10-point scale, introduced by the Numismatic Guaranty Corporation (NGC), aims to bridge the gap between numismatics and other collectible hobbies by offering a simpler, more intuitive grading system. Although it parallels the Sheldon Scale in terms of precision, it simplifies the grading process into fewer main categories, making it especially accessible for newcomers to coin collecting.

Sheldon Scale

Coins are graded on a scale from 1 to 70, with 70 being a perfect condition. This scale was developed by Dr. William Sheldon in 1949 and is known as the Sheldon Scale. The scale includes:

- Grades 1–58 cover circulated coins, with varying levels of wear.
- Grades 60–70 represent uncirculated coins, with no signs of wear.

Dr. Sheldon also used these 13 "grades" to represent the 1 to 70 scale (*Coin Grading*, 2022):

- Poor
- Fair
- Almost Good
- Good
- Very Good
- Fine
- Very Fine
- Extra Fine
- Almost Uncirculated
- Uncirculated
- Brilliant Uncirculated
- Gem Uncirculated
- Perfect Uncirculated

British Coin Grading

The British coin grading system is distinctive in its use of descriptive terms to assess the condition of coins, contrasting with the numerical Sheldon Scale more commonly used in the United States and other regions.

The British system uses several key descriptive terms to grade coins (*Discover British Coin Grading*, 2023):

- **Fine (F):** Coins show moderate to considerable wear. Details are slightly worn, and minor scratches or nicks may be present, but the design is intact and legible.
- **Very Fine (VF):** Coins exhibit less wear than those graded as Fine. They retain more of the original design features, though minor scratches or blemishes are present.
- **Extremely Fine (EF):** These coins display minimal wear, maintaining distinct design details with only minor imperfections visible upon close inspection.
- **Uncirculated (UNC):** Coins in this category have no signs of wear and maintain a sharp, lustrous appearance as if freshly minted.

This system prioritizes the visual and tactile aspects of the coin, focusing on wear and tear, the sharpness of design, the definition of effigies, and overall surface quality. This makes it highly suitable for historical British coins where the depiction of monarchs and iconic motifs is significant.

NGCX 10-Point Grading Scale

The NGCX 10-Point Grading Scale, introduced by the Numismatic Guaranty Corporation (NGC), is designed to simplify the coin grading process for a broader audience. This new scale, which consists of 29 detailed grades within a primary 10-point system, aligns closely with grading systems used in other collectibles like comics or trading cards.

- **Grades 10 to 9:** Decreases by 0.1 increments.
- **Grades 9 to 8:** Offers three specific grading options.
- **Below Grade 8:** Grades decrease by 0.5 increments.

- **Applicability:** Suitable for all modern bullion coins produced from 1982 onward.
- **NGC Guarantee:** Includes the same level of precision and reliability as NGC's traditional services. (*The NGC Introduces a New 10-Point Grading Scale for Coins*, 2023)

TOP GRADING SERVICES

Professional coin grading services evaluate the condition of coins, assigning them grades based on their preservation and quality. Collectors and dealers submit coins for grading to ensure authenticity, enhance market value, and protect investments. These services usually involve a submission process where collectors need to become members, select grading tiers, complete submission forms, and prepare their coins for secure shipping. The associated costs vary depending on the coin's value, desired turnaround time, and additional services like conservation or error verification. Turnaround times also vary, ranging from one day to several weeks, depending on the service tier selected.

Professional Coin Grading Services (PCGS)

Founded in 1986, PCGS is known for its pioneering role in standardizing coin grading through a detailed numerical scale. PCGS offers a range of services including secure encapsulation, TrueView high-quality photography, and a guarantee of grade and authenticity. Its reputation is built on reliability and precision, making it a preferred choice among serious collectors and investors. (*What Is Coin Grading and Why?*, n.d.)

Numismatic Guaranty Corporation (NGC)

Established in 1987, NGC provides coin grading and encapsulation services. Known for its rigorous grading process and strong security measures, NGC ensures the accuracy of its grades through a guarantee that extends to all coins it certifies. NGC offers various grading options and educational resources to assist collectors in understanding the grading process. (*How to Submit*, n.d.)

American Numismatic Association Certification Service (ANACS)

ANACS, the oldest of the major grading services, started in 1972 under the American Numismatic Association (ANA). It is recognized for grading a wide variety of coins, including error coins and problem coins, which are provided a "details grade" that notes significant issues. ANACS offers both a standard grading service and additional services like variety attributions and error verifications. (*Services*, n.d.)

Independent Coin Graders (ICG)

ICG is known for its efficient service and competitive pricing, which includes a range of grading tiers and rapid turnaround times. ICG grades all types of U.S. and foreign coins, providing detailed encapsulation to ensure the integrity of each coin's grade. Their open approach to accepting coins already graded by other services for regrading or crossover makes them unique. (*The Grading Process*, 2024)

HOW TO GRADE A COIN

Grading a coin accurately is crucial for understanding its value and collectibility.

Gather Your Materials

Before you begin, make sure you have the right tools. You'll need a good light source (preferably natural light or a soft white bulb), a magnifying glass (ideally with 5x to 8x magnification), and a clean, soft surface to place the coins on while examining them.

Examine the Coin's Surfaces

Start by inspecting the overall condition of the coin. Look for any signs of wear, damage, or unusual marks. Check both sides of the coin thoroughly. Use your magnifying glass to look closely at the coin's surface, focusing on any fine details that are not visible to the naked eye.

Look for Key Features

Then, identify these key aspects of the coin that affect its grade:

- **Luster:** The original shine present on uncirculated coins, which diminishes with age and wear.
- **Strike Quality:** How well the coin's design was stamped onto the blank coin. A well-struck coin will have crisp, clear details.
- **Surface Preservation:** Assess how well the coin's surface has been preserved from physical damage like scratches, dents, or corrosion.

Determine the Coin's Bucket

Coins are categorized into one of three general grades before a more specific grade is assigned:

- **Circulated:** Shows signs of wear due to being used in commerce.
- **About Uncirculated (AU):** Shows very slight wear on the highest points, often only visible under magnification.
- **Uncirculated (Mint State or MS):** No signs of wear, though it may still exhibit contact marks from minting or storage.

Select the Coin's Approximate Grade

Match your coin's condition to the appropriate descriptive grade on the scale of your choice. This will involve comparing your observations against a grading standard or chart.

Assign a Number

Assign a numerical grade based on your assessment of how the coin matches up to descriptors for each grade level. A detailed grading guide or chart will provide specific criteria for each grade.

Check Your Results

Review the grade you have assigned and compare it to professionally graded coins, if possible. This can be done by examining coins in numismatic publications, at coin shows, or online. Checking your results helps refine your grading skills and ensures accuracy. (*A Complete Coin Grading Guide for All Investing Skill Levels*, 2024; Davidson, 2023)

BUILDING YOUR GRADING SKILLS

As a coin collector, learning to grade coins accurately makes the hobby more enjoyable and protects your investments. Knowing a coin's grade helps you understand its true value, make better buying choices, and avoid paying too much based on inaccurate conditions (Thorne, 2023). This skill is key to intelligently expanding your collection and making sure every new coin is a worthwhile addition.

Practice Regularly

The cornerstone of developing any skill is consistent practice. For coin grading, this means regularly examining coins and trying to grade them. Begin with coins whose grade is already known and compare your assessments against the established grades. This practice helps in understanding the subtleties between different grades and what distinguishes them.

Study Coins of Various Grades and Conditions

Spend time studying coins of various grades and conditions to familiarize yourself with the common characteristics that define each grade. Pay special attention to key details like luster, strike quality, and signs of wear. Resources such as high-resolution photographs available in numismatic books or online, detailed grading guides, and actual graded coins can provide invaluable reference points for understanding how different conditions affect a coin's appearance and grade.

Attend Coin Shows, Workshops, or Seminars

Coin shows and seminars offer opportunities to see a wide variety of coins and interact with experienced collectors and numismatic experts. These events often include workshops or sessions focused on grading where you can learn practical tips and techniques, observe demonstrations, and ask questions directly to professionals. This direct learning experience is crucial in accelerating your understanding of grading standards.

Seek Feedback From Peers or Online Communities

Engaging with other collectors through clubs, online forums, or social media groups can provide additional learning opportunities. Sharing your graded coins and seeking feedback can open discussions that refine your grading assumptions and expose you to different perspectives. Additionally, these communities often share useful resources and can offer advice on improving grading techniques.

Utilize Advanced Tools and Technology

As you advance in your grading skills, incorporating tools like digital microscopes or specialized lighting can further enhance your ability to detect subtle flaws or attributes that are not visible to the naked eye. These tools are often used in professional grading services and can provide a deeper understanding of what factors influence a coin's grade.

Ongoing Learning and Certification

Consider pursuing formal education or certification in coin grading. Organizations like the ANA offer courses that range from beginner to advanced levels (Garrett, 2023). These courses often culminate in a certification that not only boosts your grading skills but also enhances your credibility as a collector.

SUMMARY

- **Essential Understanding of Coin Grading:** Coin grading is a systematic process that evaluates the condition of a coin to determine its grade, which impacts its market value, historical significance, and collectibility. It is vital for every collector to grasp the grading basics to enhance their collection's value and appreciation.
- **Factors Influencing Coin Grade:** Several factors affect coin grading, including wear and tear, luster, strike quality, eye appeal, and preservation. Each element plays a crucial role in determining the final grade assigned to a coin, influencing its desirability and market price.
- **Benefits of Coin Grading:** Properly graded coins often fetch higher prices due to their certified condition, which offers assurances of authenticity and quality to potential buyers. Grading also helps in appreciating the historical and aesthetic significance of a coin, making it more collectible.
- **Grading Standards and Systems:** The Sheldon Scale is the most recognized grading system in the U.S., using a numerical scale from 1 (poor) to 70 (perfect). The British grading system uses descriptive terms, focusing more on

general condition rather than precise numerical ratings. The NGCX 10-point grading scale introduced by NGC simplifies the process, making it accessible for newcomers by closely aligning with grading scales of other collectibles.

- **Professional Coin Grading Services:** Top grading services like PCGS, NGC, ANACS, and ICG offer professional grading that assesses coins based on strict standards to ensure their authenticity and condition. These services provide a valuable resource for collectors to verify the quality of their coins, which is essential for enhancing trust and value in the numismatic community.

CONCLUSION

In this chapter, you learned about the essential role of coin grading and how it affects a coin's value and desirability. We covered important factors like wear, luster, and preservation that help determine a coin's condition and market value.

Next, we'll talk about coin valuation. You'll discover what influences a coin's worth and how to accurately evaluate it. This knowledge will help you make informed choices and improve your collection. Get ready to learn practical strategies for appraising coins, boosting both your expertise and your collection's value.

7

DETERMINING THE WORTH OF YOUR COIN

Consider three of the world's most valuable coins, each encapsulating unique chapters of history:

First, let's explore the 1933 Saint-Gaudens Double Eagle, one of the most storied coins in American numismatics. This gold coin, originally valued at $20, is distinguished by its vibrant depiction of Lady Liberty striding forward with a torch in one hand and an olive branch in the other. The rarity of this coin stems from its unique history: although 445,000 were minted during the height of the Great Depression, almost all were melted down as part of the government's efforts to remove gold from circulation. Only a few escaped this fate, one of which sold for over $7 million in 2002, highlighting its incredible value to collectors.

Next, consider the 1913 Liberty Head Nickel, also known as the "V" nickel for the Roman numeral V on its reverse. Its intrigue comes from the circumstances of its creation—only five specimens were ever produced, under circumstances that remain partially shrouded in mystery. These coins were never officially released into circulation, and their existence was only made public years later. Their story is filled with tales of secretive mint employees and wealthy collectors who cherished these nickels. One of these nickels fetched more than $3.7 million at a 2010 auction, a testament to its rarity and the fascinating story behind its creation.

Lastly, delve into the medieval world with the 1343 Edward III Florin, also known as the Double Leopard. Minted in England, this coin features the majestic image of King Edward III seated on a large throne, holding the orb and scepter, symbols of royal authority. Its name, 'Double Leopard,' is derived from the two leopard heads flanking the king's portrait, a design rich in medieval symbolism. Less than three examples of this coin are known to exist today, making it extremely rare and highly valuable. It encapsulates a significant period in British history, marked by royal power and artistic achievement in coinage.

While these coins command extraordinary prices at auction, the methods used to evaluate them apply universally. This chapter will explore how the same principles of rarity, condition, and historical importance that affect these treasures can also be used to assess the value of more common coins. Whether a novice or an expert, understanding these principles will enrich your appreciation of your collection and enhance your decision-making in buying or trading coins.

IMPORTANCE OF COIN VALUATION

As a coin collector, understanding how to value your coins is crucial for several reasons (Stevens, 2023):

- **Informed Decision-Making:** First, it helps you make informed choices when buying, selling, or trading coins. This ensures you don't pay too much or sell for too little, allowing you to trade fairly and maximize your investment returns.
- **Assessment of Collection Worth:** Second, knowing the value of your collection is vital for insurance purposes or estate planning. With an accurate assessment of what your coins are worth, you can protect your investments and manage your financial and legal affairs effectively.
- **Market Trends Insight:** Third, grasping how to value coins gives you insight into the market trends within the numismatic community. Understanding how the value of specific coins changes over time helps you make strategic decisions and take advantage of current market opportunities.

FACTORS INFLUENCING COIN VALUE

The primary factors that influence the value of coins include rarity, grade/condition, demand, design, bullion content, and historical significance. Understanding these factors can help collectors and investors make informed decisions and potentially find underappreciated coins that might appreciate in value over time. Here's how each factor contributes to a coin's value:

Rarity

The rarity of a coin significantly affects its value. Coins that were minted in limited quantities or have unique variations due to errors or special circumstances tend to be more valuable. The fewer coins available, the more collectors may be willing to pay to acquire them.

Grade/Condition

The condition of a coin is crucial in determining its value. Coins in better condition, showing little to no wear and maintaining most of their original luster, are valued higher. Coin grading services evaluate the condition using a detailed scale, from Poor to Mint State, which helps establish a coin's market value. Coins in slabs have typically been graded and authenticated by professional grading services. The slab includes a label detailing the coin's grade, type, and other relevant information, confirming its condition and authenticity. A coin slab is a protective, sealed hard plastic container used primarily for storing and displaying valuable coins.

Demand

The level of collector interest in a specific coin or series can drive up its value. Popular coins or those belonging to a beloved series often command higher prices, while less sought-after coins might not appreciate as much.

Design

The aesthetic appeal of a coin can also influence its desirability. Unique or historically significant designs can attract more interest from collectors, thereby increasing a coin's value. This includes coins with artistic merit or those that feature significant figures or events.

Bullion Content

The intrinsic value of the metals (like gold or silver) used in a coin can also determine its worth. Coins made from precious metals typically have a base value tied to the current market price of those metals, which can fluctuate based on economic factors.

Historical Significance

Coins with a rich historical background or those minted during significant historical events are often valued higher due to their historical importance. Collectors value the story and the context of the coin as much as the item itself, which can greatly enhance its collectibility and market value. (Spurrier, 2021)

HOW TO DETERMINE COIN VALUE

Determining the value of your coins is as important as it is rewarding. Whether you're a seasoned numismatist or just starting out, understanding the worth of your coins can profoundly influence your decisions and strategies in collecting.

Physical Examination

To assess a coin's value, start with a thorough physical examination. This includes checking the coin's condition, rarity, and any unique features. Use a magnifying glass to inspect for any wear and tear, scratches, or unique markings. Authenticating and grading the coin are crucial steps in this process. Professional grading services like PCGS or NGC can certify the coin's authenticity and condition, providing a standardized grade that is critical for determining its value accurately (Garrett, 2022).

In addition to the basic physical examination techniques such as using a magnifying glass to inspect a coin's surface, numismatists also recommend employing more nuanced approaches to fully appreciate and evaluate a coin. For instance, adopting a systematic method like the 'coin-and-clock' technique can be extremely beneficial. By viewing the top of the coin as 12 o'clock and then methodically examining the coin's surface in a clockwise direction, collectors can uncover even the most subtle flaws or features that might influence a coin's value. This process involves tilting and rotating the coin to scrutinize both its obverse and reverse, ensuring that no detail is overlooked. By integrating this meticulous examination method, collectors not only enhance their ability to assess the coin's condition accurately but also deepen their appreciation for its aesthetic and historical significance.

How to look at coins:

- **Appreciate the Beauty:** One of the most enjoyable aspects of coin collecting is appreciating each coin's beauty. This could be its patina, the quality of its strike, or the artistry in its design. Remember, every coin you add to your collection has its own unique appeal.
- **Identify Positive Attributes:** Own your coins with pride by recognizing their best features, like outstanding toning or sharp details. This will not only enhance your satisfaction as a collector but could also increase the coin's value if you decide to sell.
- **Spot Imperfections:** Always keep an eye out for any flaws. These imperfections can help you negotiate a lower price, ensuring you don't overpay. Remember,

missing these can lead to paying more than the coin is worth.

- **Assess Strengths and Weaknesses:** Evaluate your coins impartially by identifying what contributes to their grading, whether it's the eye appeal, luster, or overall strike. Understanding these factors helps you grasp the true value of each coin.
- **Use the Coin-and-Clock Method:** Imagine the coin as a clock face when examining it. Start from the top (12 o'clock) and inspect it methodically in a circle. This technique helps you catch details you might otherwise miss.
- **Look for Unique Varieties:** Keep an eye out for coins with unique errors or features, as these can be quite valuable. Tools like *The Cherrypickers' Guide* can be invaluable for spotting these special varieties.
- **Seek Upgrades:** Sometimes coins in your collection might be eligible for a higher grade, which could significantly increase their value. Learning to identify such opportunities can be quite profitable.
- **Check for Wear:** Despite a coin being graded by a reputable service, it's wise to inspect for any signs of wear yourself. This ensures you know exactly what you are getting, as even slight wear can affect a coin's classification.
- **Match Toning for Sets:** When collecting sets of coins, try to find pieces that have similar toning. This not only enhances the aesthetic appeal but also adds to the collection's value.
- **Watch for Deterioration:** Regularly check your coins for any signs of deterioration, such as unusual coloration or

damage. If you spot something, acting quickly can prevent long-term degradation and loss of value.

Research and Market Comparisons

To accurately determine the current market value of your coin, it's essential to engage in thorough research. Start by checking recent sales and auction results to see how similar coins are valued. Focus on reputable sources such as well-recognized auction houses and established numismatic websites that publish sales data. Utilize published price guides, which are updated regularly and reflect current market conditions. These guides are available both online and in print, offering a comprehensive overview of coin values based on grade and rarity.

In addition to traditional price guides, explore specialized coin valuation websites and coin management apps (*How Much Is Your Collection Worth*, n.d.). These platforms provide dynamic, up-to-date pricing and market trends, often tailored to the specifics of your coin type and condition. Make sure to compare your coin to similar ones recently sold or currently listed in the market—this comparison helps establish a baseline value.

When researching, always cross-reference multiple sources to ensure accuracy and avoid reliance on potentially outdated or biased information. By comparing your coin against similar ones, assessing their sale prices, and consulting various reputable resources, you can establish a well-informed estimate of what your coin might realistically fetch in a sale, ensuring you are well-prepared for either buying or selling.

Websites for Coin Valuation

- **Coin Value Checker** - Provides a comprehensive tool for evaluating US coins, integrating data from authoritative sources like PCGS and Coin World, and offering insights into numismatic articles and coin collecting basics.
- **PCGS CoinFacts** - Offers a detailed online guide with information on over 25,000 US and world coins, including images, mintage figures, significant auctions, and a range of prices based on actual coin grading.
- **NGC Coin Price Guide** - Powered by Numismatic Guaranty Corporation, this guide provides market-researched values for coins, searchable by country, category, series, date, and grade.
- **Numista** - Features a vast online community with a catalog offering specifications, images, discussion forums, and a price estimator for over 100,000 coins from around the world.
- **Coinappraiser** - This site offers detailed information and values for over 10,000 US and world coins and provides a tool for submitting coins for professional appraisal.

Apps for Coin Management and Value Checking

- **PCGS CoinFacts App** - Access an extensive electronic coin catalog, explore auctions, and get up-to-date information on over 39,000 pieces.
- **NGC App** - Connect with a global community of coin collectors, find rare coins, determine their worth, and explore specialized dealers.

- **CoinManage** - A comprehensive database featuring various coins by Mintmark, denomination, and country of origin, helpful for managing collections.
- **CoinSnap** - Determine the value of any coin by uploading a photo and gain insights about its origin and rarity.

Consult Experts

Consulting knowledgeable professionals, such as certified coin appraisers or numismatics organizations, is crucial in accurately assessing your coin collection. Professional appraisers, armed with expertise in numismatics, conduct a thorough evaluation of your coins considering factors such as historical significance, rarity, and condition. They utilize a variety of methods to appraise coins, including direct comparison with market values and detailed physical examinations.

When you choose a professional appraisal, it provides a clear, objective valuation based on market research and expert observations. This process often involves checking the physical condition of each coin, verifying authenticity, and comparing it against current market prices and auction records. This comprehensive approach allows appraisers to offer you detailed insights and a realistic view of your collection's market potential, which is invaluable if you consider selling or insuring your coins.

By obtaining a professional appraisal, you not only gain an accurate understanding of your collection's worth but also receive guidance on potential areas for action, such as improving the collection's insurance coverage based on the appraised values or making informed decisions about buying or selling specific pieces. The appraisal process also helps in recognizing any rare gems within your collection that might carry exceptional value, often overlooked in general assessments.

A proper appraisal will document each coin's value, providing you with a reliable record that can be used for insurance purposes, future sales, or family inheritance planning. The credibility that comes with a professional appraisal also adds to your collection's provenance, making it more desirable in the numismatic community.

To ensure the best results from your appraisal, opt for appraisers who are certified by reputable bodies such as the American Numismatic Association or have substantial positive testimonials reflecting their expertise and reliability (Stevens, 2023b). Engaging with a professional who offers transparent and communicative evaluations can significantly enhance your understanding and appreciation of your coin collection's true worth.

Attend Coin Shows and Exhibitions

Coin shows and exhibitions provide a platform for engaging directly with experts and gaining firsthand insights into the coin collecting world. At a coin show, you can receive immediate feedback on your coins, discuss grading nuances, and learn about the latest market trends that could affect your collecting or selling strategies.

For those new to coin collecting, local coin shows are an excellent starting point. They allow you to familiarize yourself with the coin collecting community in a more manageable setting compared to larger national events, which might feel overwhelming at first. At these shows, you can meet club members who often serve as dealers or fellow buyers, adding a sense of familiarity and easing your integration into the numismatic community. This environment encourages learning and exchange, providing you with the knowledge needed to navigate the hobby more effectively.

Moreover, coin shows are an ideal venue for building relationships that could prove beneficial for future transactions. The camaraderie and shared passion for numismatics foster a unique learning environment. You are encouraged to ask questions, whether about the specifics of a coin or about numismatics in general. Many dealers are eager to share their knowledge and might even offer insights into particular pieces, enhancing your understanding and appreciation of your collection.

As you navigate your first coin show, remember to take your time. Explore the booths, engage with the sellers, and observe the interactions. Bring along a loupe or magnifying glass to closely examine coins, as recommended by experts, to better appreciate their condition and fine details. Approach each interaction with courtesy and respect, which not only helps in building meaningful connections but also enriches your overall experience at the show.

By actively participating in coin shows and exhibitions, you not only expand your knowledge and network but also deepen your engagement with the hobby, potentially uncovering unique pieces to enhance your collection.

Reassess Regularly

Regular reassessment of your coin collection's value is crucial due to the dynamic nature of the numismatic market. Fluctuations in market conditions, collector demand, and numismatic trends significantly impact coin values. For instance, recent trends have shown considerable price increases for both circulated and Mint State coins, driven by a renewed interest in rare coins as alternative investments and inflation hedges. Additionally, rare U.S. coins have seen price escalations, as exemplified by a significant auction where an ancient Greek gold stater fetched nearly $6 million, suggesting a rising market valuation for such rarities.

To stay abreast of these changes, it's important to monitor reliable sources that report on coin market trends, such as the PCGS Price Guide which offers updated information on price changes across various coin series. This guide allows collectors to track the top gainers and losers in price, helping them understand which segments of their collection are appreciating or depreciating. Attending auctions not only provides insights into current collector preferences but also showcases the economic factors influencing coin values, giving you a comprehensive view of the market (Bozarth & Ferguson, 2021).

This ongoing reassessment process ensures that your valuation remains accurate, allowing you to make informed decisions whether you're buying, selling, or simply holding onto your coins. Understanding these market dynamics can help you strategically time your transactions to maximize returns or minimize losses, reflecting the ever-evolving landscape of coin collecting.

SUMMARY

- **Informed Decision-Making:** Valuing coins accurately helps collectors make educated choices in buying, selling, or trading coins, ensuring fair transactions and maximizing investment returns.
- **Understanding Collection Worth:** Knowing the value of a coin collection aids in managing insurance and estate planning, providing security for the collector's investment.
- **Insight Into Market Trends:** Grasping the valuation of coins offers insights into numismatic market trends, enabling strategic buying or selling decisions based on how the value of specific coins change over time.
- **Factors Influencing Coin Value:** The value of a coin is influenced by several factors including rarity, condition, demand, design, bullion content, and historical significance. Each of these aspects plays a critical role in determining a coin's market value.
- **Determining Coin Value:** To determine a coin's value, collectors should engage in physical examination, research market comparisons, consult experts, attend coin shows, and regularly reassess their collection to keep up with market changes and ensure accurate valuations.

CONCLUSION

In this chapter, we've uncovered the importance of accurately valuing coins, which aids in making informed decisions, protecting investments, and understanding market trends. Key factors like rarity, condition, demand, and historical significance play essential roles in determining a coin's worth.

As we move forward, the next chapter will guide you through proper coin handling, cleaning, and preservation techniques. You'll learn to maintain and potentially enhance the value of your collection, ensuring its longevity and appeal for years to come.

8

HANDLING AND CLEANING COINS SAFELY

Imagine a novice coin collector excitedly purchasing their first rare coin—an exquisite 1909-S VDB Lincoln Cent, prized for its rarity and historical significance. Eager to examine their new treasure, they handle the coin directly with bare fingers. Within moments, the grim reality sets in as they notice faint smudges and scratches marring the once pristine surface of this valuable piece.

Now, consider another collector who, in an attempt to enhance the shine of an old silver dollar, decides to use a common household cleaner. Despite their good intentions, the abrasive solution leaves irreversible chemical stains and etches on the coin's delicate surface, ruining an artifact that had survived over a century in remarkable condition.

This is the art and science of maintaining the pristine condition of coins. Our goal is to arm you with the knowledge and techniques necessary to avoid the common pitfalls that can lead to the kind of heartbreak our novice collectors experienced. By understanding the best practices for handling and cleaning your coins, you can preserve their historical, aesthetic, and monetary value. Join us as we explore how to treat these tiny pieces of history with the respect they deserve, ensuring they remain intact for future generations to cherish.

HANDLING COINS PROPERLY

Coin collecting is not just a pastime—it's a preservation of history, culture, and art. Each coin carries stories from the past, from monumental economic changes to tales of old civilizations (*Why Is It Important to Handle Coins Properly?*, 2015). But beyond their historical and aesthetic value, coins, particularly rare and uncirculated ones, possess significant monetary value. It is crucial, therefore, that they are handled with utmost care to maintain their condition and value.

Coins are remarkably delicate artifacts. Their surfaces, especially those that are proof or uncirculated, can be easily marred by fingerprints, oils, and even the slightest abrasion, each of which can significantly diminish their value. Handling coins improperly is akin to erasing pages from a history book—once the damage is done, it cannot be undone.

The importance of handling coins properly cannot be overstated. By touching a coin directly with bare skin, natural oils and minute dirt particles from the skin can transfer to the coin. This not only tarnishes its appearance but can lead to chemical reactions with the metal, leading to spots, corrosion, and other damage that irreparably affects the coin's numismatic value. For instance, pure gold coins, like the American Gold Buffalo, are highly susceptible to damage from even the smallest mishandlings due to their soft metal composition.

Similarly, rare coins with mirror-like finishes that add to their allure can lose their illustrious sheen if mishandled. Storing such coins in improper materials like PVC holders can also cause damage over time due to the emission of harmful chemicals under certain conditions, such as heat and light exposure (Stevens, 2023a).

BEST PRACTICES FOR HANDLING COINS

Handling coins properly is an essential part of coin collecting that preserves the physical condition and historical integrity of each piece. By treating each coin with the care it deserves, collectors ensure that these tiny pieces of history are preserved for future generations to study and appreciate. Adopting these practices as part of your routine when interacting with your coin collection will not only maintain the aesthetic and historical value of the coins but also enhance their longevity and worth as collectibles:

- **Clean Hands:** It's imperative to wash and dry your hands thoroughly before handling coins. This step removes oils, dirt, and debris that can transfer to a coin's surface, potentially causing damage. Ensuring your hands are clean minimizes the risk of leaving fingerprints or other residues that can tarnish or chemically react with the surface of the coin.
- **Cotton Gloves:** Wearing cotton gloves or using soft, lint-free cloths when handling coins can greatly reduce the risk of direct contact with the skin. This practice is particularly important when dealing with rare or highly valuable coins as it prevents oils and acids from the skin from damaging the coin's surface. Gloves also prevent fingerprints, which can be difficult to remove

and detract from the coin's aesthetic and numismatic value.
- **Minimal Contact:** Whenever possible, handle coins by their edges or rims and avoid touching their faces. This method of handling is crucial as it minimizes the potential for damage and contamination. The oils and minute debris from your fingers can adhere to the coin's surface, leading to tarnishing and potential chemical reactions that can degrade the coin over time.
- **Soft Surfaces:** Always place coins on clean, soft surfaces such as a velvet pad or a soft cloth when examining or displaying them. This precaution prevents scratches or abrasions from rough or uneven surfaces, which can be particularly detrimental to the coin's finish and overall appearance.
- **Avoiding Harsh Chemicals:** Never use abrasive cleaners, solvents, or chemicals on coins. These substances can cause irreversible damage to the surfaces and finishes of the coins. For cleaning, it is best to consult a professional or use only mild soaps and ensure thorough rinsing and drying to avoid leaving residues that could damage the coin over time. (*6 Rules for Properly Handling Your Precious Metal Coins*, 2019; *Why Is It Important to Handle Coins Properly?*, 2015)

WHY YOU SHOULD NOT CLEAN COINS

Cleaning coins might seem like a straightforward way to enhance their appearance, but it is generally advised against due to the potential damage it can cause. Here are several reasons why cleaning coins is usually not recommended (McMorrow-Hernandez, n.d.):

- **Loss of Numismatic Value:** Coins, especially those that are rare or have historical significance, carry value that extends beyond their material worth. The natural patina that develops over time on coins is considered part of their character and history. Cleaning a coin often removes this patina, significantly diminishing its numismatic value and collector appeal. Collectors prefer coins in their original, unaltered state, and cleaned coins are often worth less than their uncleaned counterparts.
- **Risk of Physical Damage:** Many cleaning methods, even those that might seem gentle, can cause irreversible damage to the coin's surface. Abrasive cleaning agents, such as toothpaste, baking soda, or even mild soaps, can leave microscopic scratches on the coin, altering its finish and luster. Harsh chemicals can react with the metals in the coin, causing discoloration and permanent marks that detract from the coin's appearance and value.
- **Deterioration of Historical Integrity:** Each coin tells a story and carries the marks of its journey through time. By cleaning a coin, you may inadvertently erase these historical markers. For instance, the handling marks, toning, and even the small dings or scratches all contribute to the historical narrative of the coin. Cleaning these away can result in a loss of the very essence that makes a coin particularly valuable to collectors and historians.
- **Potential for Misleading Appearance:** Cleaned coins can sometimes be made to look newer than they actually are, which can mislead potential buyers about the age and true condition of the coin. This can be particularly problematic in the trading and selling of coins, where authenticity and original condition are highly valued.

- **Long-Term Preservation Issues:** Improper cleaning can expose a coin to elements that accelerate deterioration. For example, removing a coin's tarnish or patina might expose the underlying metal to more aggressive oxidation or corrosion in the future, leading to more serious damage than if it had been left in its original state.

CLEANING COINS SAFELY

Cleaning a coin not only risks damaging the coin physically and diminishing its value but also disrupts the historical integrity that adds so much to its appeal and worth. If cleaning is absolutely necessary, it should only be performed by professionals who understand the delicate nature of the task and can minimize potential harm.

For collectors who decide to clean their coins despite the risks involved, it is crucial to follow safe cleaning practices to minimize potential damage. Here's a guide to safely cleaning coins using three different methods: gentle washing, mechanical cleaning, and chemical cleaning.

Gentle Washing

Gentle washing is a basic method suitable for all types of coins to remove surface dirt and grime without aggressive chemicals.

Steps:

1. Fill a bowl with lukewarm water and add a few drops of mild soap.

2. Submerge the coins in the soapy water and let them soak for a few minutes to loosen the dirt.
3. Remove the coins one at a time, and use a soft brush (like a baby toothbrush) to gently scrub the surface.
4. Rinse each coin under running lukewarm water to remove any soap residue.
5. Dry the coins with a soft, lint-free cloth by patting them gently. Allow them to air dry on a clean towel. (*How NOT to Clean Coins*, 2013)

Mechanical Cleaning

Mechanical cleaning involves using non-abrasive tools to physically remove stubborn dirt or deposits without damaging the coin's surface.

Steps:

1. Use a soft brush to remove loose dirt. For more stubborn grime, you can use a toothpick or a soft dental pick, carefully avoiding scratching the coin's surface.
2. For tough spots, use a rubber eraser gently over the affected area to lift dirt.
3. If using a toothpick or dental pick, cover the coin's surface with masking tape to protect it from accidental scratches. Only expose the part you are cleaning. (*Coin Cleaning*, 2022)

Chemical Cleaning

Chemical cleaning should be used as a last resort due to the risks of altering the coin's patina and potentially damaging its surface.

Steps:

1. Use acetone for coins that are not overly sensitive. Submerge the coin in a small container filled with acetone, ensuring the area is well-ventilated.
2. Let the coin soak for a few minutes, then remove it and gently pat dry with a soft cloth.
3. For more ingrained dirt, a diluted solution of mild dish soap and water can be used. Soak the coin, then clean gently with a soft brush and rinse thoroughly.
4. Always handle coins with gloves when using chemicals to avoid further contamination and to protect your skin. (Lyons, 2024)

Important Precautions

- Always test the cleaning method on a less valuable coin first to ensure it does not damage the coin.
- Avoid over-cleaning. Strive to maintain the coin's original appearance as much as possible.
- Consult with a professional if you are unsure about the coin's material and how it might react to different cleaning methods.

UNDERSTANDING COIN DAMAGE

Coin damage occurs through a variety of mechanisms, each capable of significantly impacting a coin's appearance and numismatic value. The primary culprits include exposure to environmental elements such as air, moisture, and pollutants.

Oxidation, a common issue due to air exposure, affects coins made from reactive metals like copper and silver, leading to patina or tarnish. While sometimes aesthetically valued, excessive tarnish can obscure critical details, detracting from the coin's value. Moisture poses similar threats, causing corrosion that is particularly prevalent in humid environments or places with fluctuating temperatures (*Photos of Damaged Coins*, 2022).

Chemicals found in everyday handling and cleaning products can also damage coins. Acids and harsh solvents might strip protective layers off the coins, altering their appearance and diminishing their value (Headley, 2021b). Environmental pollutants and even small amounts of substances transferred by human touch can accelerate this degradation, making the handling and cleaning of coins a delicate task that requires proper knowledge to avoid introducing irreversible damage.

In addition, improper storage solutions contribute significantly to potential damage. For instance, storing coins in PVC holders can lead to harmful chemical reactions, while paper and cardboard storage materials, if not acid-free, might emit damaging acids over time. Such environments facilitate the deterioration process, underscoring the importance of proper coin handling and storage to preserve their integrity and value.

COIN DAMAGE OR MINT ERRORS?

While both coin damage and mint errors affect a coin's appearance, their implications for value and collectibility are vastly different.

Mint Errors

Mint errors are anomalies that occur during the coin minting process, resulting in coins that deviate from their intended design or specifications. These errors are generally classified into categories based on the stage of the minting process during which they occur: planchet errors, die errors, and striking errors. Planchet errors might include issues like clipped or improperly sized planchets. Die errors can involve doubled dies or missing design elements, while strike errors cover incidents like off-center or double strikes (*Types of Coin Damage and Mint Errors*, 2023).

Mint errors are sought after by collectors due to their rarity and the unique stories they tell about the minting process. These errors can significantly increase a coin's value because they add a level of scarcity and uniqueness to the coin.

Post Mint Damage (PMD) and Post Strike Damage (PSD)

Contrasting with mint errors, Post Mint Damage (PMD) or Post Strike Damage (PSD) refers to any damage that occurs after the coin has been struck and has left the mint (Sullivan, 2022). This can include wear from circulation, environmental damage such as corrosion or tarnishing, and damage from improper handling like scratches or cleaning.

While mint errors enhance a coin's value due to their rarity and unique characteristics, PMD usually detracts from a coin's value, making it less desirable to collectors. PMD represents the typical wear and tear that coins undergo once they enter circulation or are improperly stored.

Assessing Coin Condition

- **Initial Inspection:** Examine the coin closely, preferably with magnification, to observe any irregularities or deviations from standard coinage. This can help identify obvious signs of PMD such as scratches, dents, or corrosion.
- **Research:** Utilize numismatic resources such as books, websites, and community forums to understand common characteristics of both mint errors and types of damage. This knowledge can aid in distinguishing peculiarities that are the result of errors during the minting process from those caused by external factors.
- **Consult Experts:** For a definitive assessment, consult professionals such as numismatists or reputable coin grading services. These experts can provide valuable insights based on their experience and the diagnostic tools they use, which can definitively categorize the nature of the irregularity as a mint error or post-mint damage. (Sepanek, 2024)

WHAT TO DO WITH DAMAGED COINS

Handling damaged coins can be a dilemma for collectors. While such coins may have reduced numismatic value, there are several viable options for managing them effectively.

Clean the Coins for Your Personal Collection

If the coins are not of significant numismatic value but hold personal value or interest, cleaning them for display or personal collection might be a good option. This should be done carefully to avoid further damage. For basic cleaning, soaking the coins in a gentle soap solution and using a soft brush can be effective.

Send Them to the U.S. Mint

The U.S. Mint operates a Mutilated Coin Redemption Program that compensates collectors for damaged coins based on the bullion value rather than face value. This is particularly beneficial for precious metal coins like gold and silver, where the intrinsic metal value is significant. It's important to check the current guidelines and procedures of the Mint before sending coins.

Exchange Coins at a Bank for Face Value

For coins that are damaged but still recognizable, banks may accept them at face value. The Federal Reserve also accepts deposits of worn coins, which they eventually cull from circulation. This option is straightforward and doesn't require coins to be sent away or assessed for precious metal content.

Trade With Coin Dealers

Coin dealers often buy damaged coins at a value based on their metal content, especially for bullion coins. They may also be interested in rare coins where numismatic value exceeds the bullion worth, even if the coin is damaged. This can sometimes yield a better return than exchanging them at face value.

Additional Considerations

- When deciding on cleaning or trading coins, it's crucial to understand the type of damage and the coin's

material. For instance, abrasive cleaning methods should be avoided for soft metals like gold, which are easily scratched.
- For collectors, the decision to clean or sell damaged coins might depend on the nature of their collection goals—whether they value aesthetic perfection or historical authenticity. (*What to Do with Mutilated Currency*, 2017)

SUMMARY

- **Proper Handling to Preserve Value:** Handling coins properly is crucial to maintaining their historical, aesthetic, and monetary value. This involves clean hands, minimal contact, and using soft surfaces for placement to avoid physical and chemical damage.
- **Risks of Cleaning Coins:** Cleaning coins is generally discouraged as it can lead to a loss of numismatic value by removing the natural patina and possibly causing physical damage that diminishes the coin's appeal and collector value.
- **Identifying Damage vs. Mint Errors:** Distinguishing between post-mint damage and mint errors is vital. Mint errors occur during the production process and can increase a coin's value, whereas post-mint damage typically decreases a coin's value.
- **Options for Damaged Coins:** For coins that are no longer in mint condition, options include cleaning for personal collections, exchanging at banks for face value, sending to the U.S. Mint for redemption, or trading with coin dealers for their intrinsic metal value.

- **Preventative Measures for Coin Longevity:**
  Implementing best practices such as using cotton gloves, handling by the edges, and avoiding harsh chemicals are all preventative measures that help maintain a coin's condition over time and prevent common types of damage.

CONCLUSION

In this chapter, we've delved into the art of coin handling; the critical importance of preserving the intricate details and historical significance of each piece in your collection. Remember, every coin is a tangible piece of history, and improper handling is like erasing chapters from history's narrative. The potential monetary loss is significant, but the loss of the coin's story and its historical context is immeasurable.

Now, as we anticipate the next chapter, we will transition from the nuanced specifics of handling to the broader, yet equally vital, considerations of storage. We'll talk about how to choose the right environment for your coins, how to organize them effectively, and which security measures will best safeguard your collection against the unexpected. How can the environment affect your coins? What might be the consequences of disorganization? What risks could your collection face, and how can you mitigate them? These questions and more will be addressed in our next chapter, ensuring that your collection can withstand the test of time—both physically and historically.

9

STORING AND ORGANIZING YOUR COIN COLLECTION

As coin collectors, we do more than gather old coins; we protect pieces of history. Each coin in your collection provides a look into a different time and carries stories that are important across generations. Our job is to keep these historical items safe, ensuring they can be appreciated by future historians and collectors. By carefully storing each coin, we maintain their stories and value for years to come.

Proper storage is crucial because it preserves the appearance and value of your coins. Moisture, changes in temperature, and air exposure can damage coins. For instance, moisture can lead to rust and discoloration, temperature changes can cause the coins to tarnish, and air can speed up their aging. To prevent this, it's important to store coins in airtight containers that are free from harmful chemicals like PVC and acids.

Renowned collectors, such as the illustrious King Farouk of Egypt, who amassed one of the most famous coin collections in the world, took meticulous steps to protect his treasures. He employed elaborate storage systems, using custom-made cabinets and safes that controlled both humidity and exposure to light. This level of care not only preserved the physical condition of his coins but also maintained their aesthetic and historical integrity, serving as a prime example for modern collectors.

Using the right storage helps keep the coins' unique details and their historical and monetary value intact. By controlling the storage environment—keeping a consistent temperature and humidity, and protecting the coins from light and poor air quality—we make sure our coin collections stay vibrant and valuable, not just now but for future generations as well.

IMPORTANCE OF PROPER STORAGE

The preservation of a coin collection is largely dependent on how it is stored. Proper storage is critical not only for maintaining the aesthetic appeal of each piece but also for preserving their value over time. Several environmental factors such as moisture, temperature fluctuations, and exposure to air significantly impact the condition of coins.

- **Moisture:** Coins are particularly susceptible to moisture, which can cause tarnishing and corrosion. Moisture can seep into storage areas during humid conditions or changes in weather, directly affecting the metal of coins and leading to potential damage.
- **Temperature Fluctuations:** Coins need to be stored in a stable environment as fluctuations in temperature can lead to condensation and increase the risk of oxidation, which may result in tarnishing. According to expert

advice, the ideal temperature for storing coins is below 75 degrees Fahrenheit.
- **Exposure to Air:** Oxygen can be one of the biggest enemies of metal preservation. Prolonged exposure to air can lead to oxidation, which affects the coin's surface and overall integrity. Therefore, ensuring coins are stored in airtight containers can prevent the natural aging process that air exposure accelerates. (*How to Store Coins Safely*, 2023)

Think about stories of ancient coins unearthed in shipwrecks or buried hoards, where elements like saltwater and soil have drastically altered their appearance and diminished their value. A notable example includes the Spanish treasure fleet wrecked off the Florida coast in 1715. Many coins recovered were heavily corroded due to centuries of exposure to saltwater, illustrating how improper natural storage over time can impact the value and legibility of historically significant coins. Similarly, some modern materials like silicone are not ideal for coin storage as it does not provide the necessary inert properties to prevent chemical reactions that could tarnish or damage the coins, potentially affecting their historical and monetary worth.

Proper storage isn't just about protecting coins from physical damage; it's also about preserving the intricate details that make each coin unique and valuable. Use PVC-free, acid-free containers such as coin folders or albums that do not emit harmful chemicals that could react with metal and degrade the coins.

Maintaining the right environment and using the correct storage materials can make a significant difference in the life and value of a coin collection. Each step taken to protect a coin from these environmental factors ensures that the collection can be enjoyed by future generations, maintaining both its monetary value and historical significance.

CHOOSING THE RIGHT STORAGE ENVIRONMENT

Preserving the integrity and value of a coin collection is largely dependent on the environment in which the coins are stored. Factors such as temperature, humidity, light exposure, and air quality can significantly influence the condition of your coins over time.

From an investment perspective, the condition of a coin significantly influences its market value. Proper storage plays a crucial role in this, as even minor improvements in a coin's condition can translate to substantial differences in its market price. For instance, a coin graded "Mint State-63" might be worth considerably more if stored in conditions that elevate its grade to "Mint State-65." Effective storage solutions, therefore, not only preserve the historical and aesthetic value of coins but can also enhance their investment potential.

Temperature and Humidity Control

Maintaining a stable environment with moderate temperature and humidity levels is crucial to prevent the deterioration of coins. Extreme temperatures can cause metals to expand and contract, which may lead to microscopic fractures and tarnishing over time. Similarly, high humidity levels can accelerate the oxidation process, leading to corrosion, especially for coins made of copper and silver.

Aim to keep the storage area at a consistent temperature below 75 degrees Fahrenheit and a humidity level around 50% (*How to Store Coins Safely*, 2022). This can often be achieved using a climate-controlled room or a storage area equipped with a dehumidifier.

Protection From Light

Exposure to direct sunlight and even strong artificial light can cause significant damage to coins over time. UV rays can fade and discolor the surfaces of coins, and prolonged exposure can even alter the chemical composition of the metals.

Store coins in a dark place such as a drawer, cabinet, or safe where light cannot penetrate. If coins are displayed, ensure they are kept in cases that block UV light or in areas away from direct sunlight and harsh indoor lighting (*How to Store Coins*, n.d.).

Air Quality

The air quality in the storage area plays a significant role in the preservation of coins. Pollutants, dust, and volatile organic compounds can accelerate tarnishing and corrosion. Poor air circulation can also trap these pollutants around the coins, increasing the risk of damage.

Ensure good air circulation in the storage area to prevent the buildup of harmful gases. Use air purifiers if necessary to maintain clean air around the collection. Additionally, it is advisable to store coins in well-sealed containers that prevent the ingress of polluted air and dust.

CONSIDERATIONS FOR CHOOSING COIN STORAGE

Choosing the right storage for your coin collection involves balancing protection with practicality. By considering the material, size, durability, and visibility of storage options, you can ensure that your coins remain in excellent condition while still being enjoyable to collect and display.

For many collectors, coin collecting is a legacy passed down through generations, and effective storage is vital in preserving this heritage. By utilizing archival-quality materials and proper environmental controls, collectors ensure that their coins maintain their condition and continue to tell their stories to future generations. Such practices underscore the role of coin collectors as custodians of historical treasures, safeguarding them not just for personal enjoyment but as part of a familial tradition that educates and inspires.

As technology advances, so do options for storing coins more effectively. Modern collectors can utilize climate-controlled display cases that not only prevent environmental damage but also beautifully showcase their coins. These high-tech storage solutions often feature UV-protective glass and temperature control, providing an optimal environment that can be finely tuned to the needs of particularly sensitive or valuable coins.

Material

The choice of material needs to be inert and non-reactive to ensure the long-term preservation of the coins. Options include:

- **Acid-Free Paper:** Ideal for envelopes and holders, preventing chemical reactions that can tarnish or corrode coins.
- **Archival-Quality Plastics:** Such as polyester or polypropylene, which do not release harmful chemicals over time, unlike PVC, which can degrade and emit acids harmful to coins.
- **Inert Metals Like Aluminum:** Aluminum cases can provide sturdy and safe housing for coins, protecting them from physical damage while also being chemically inert.
- **Silica Gel:** Look into silica gel packets for added moisture control inside storage containers, particularly in humid climates.

Size and Capacity

Select storage that accommodates the size and denomination of your coins without forcing them into tight spaces or allowing too much movement, which can lead to wear and tear:

- **Appropriate Sizing:** Ensure that the storage medium fits the specific dimensions of each coin type, preventing them from moving around and getting scratched.

- **Scalable Solutions:** Consider scalability, especially if you plan to grow your collection over time. Options that allow for easy expansion without compromising protection and organization are ideal.
- **Customizable Inserts:** Use foam inserts that can be cut to the specific sizes of unusual or irregularly shaped coins for added protection.

Durability

Choose storage options that offer durability and will protect coins over long periods:

- **Sturdy Construction:** Seek out storage options made with high-quality materials that can handle wear and tear from regular use.
- **Protective Coatings:** Consider storage options with corrosion-resistant finishes or treatments, especially for metal storage solutions, to enhance their longevity and appearance.
- **Reinforced Cases:** For high-value coins, use reinforced cases with locks or tamper-proof seals for added security and durability.

Visibility

For ease of viewing and appreciation of your coins, opt for storage solutions that allow you to see the coins without needing to handle them frequently:

- **Clear Enclosures:** Use crystal-clear enclosures for individual coins or sets that allow unobstructed viewing from all angles.
- **Display Cases:** Invest in professionally made display cases with UV-protective glass to prevent fading and deterioration from light exposure.
- **Lighting Considerations:** For display cases, consider installing LED lighting that does not emit UV light, which can damage coins over time.

(*Choosing the Right Storage to Protect Coin Values*, 2014)

MAINTAINING ORGANIZATION AND ACCESSIBILITY

Keeping your coin collection organized and accessible improves its look, makes it easier to manage, and helps you enjoy and appreciate your coins more. Here's how to keep everything in order and easy to reach:

Labeling

Labeling is crucial for quickly identifying and retrieving coins within a collection. Proper labels should include detailed information such as coin type, denomination, date, and mint mark. This not only aids in organization but also enriches the display and educational value of the collection for anyone viewing it.

Use labels that are clear and resistant to aging. Place labels on coin holders, albums, or storage boxes in a standardized format to maintain consistency across your collection.

Cataloging

A detailed inventory or catalog of your coin collection serves as a vital record of the key attributes of each coin, including condition, purchase price, and provenance. Cataloging helps in tracking the growth and value of your collection over time and makes it easier to manage for investment or inheritance purposes.

Depending on the size of your collection, use either a physical notebook, digital spreadsheets, or specialized coin collection software. It's advisable to keep backups of digital records to prevent data loss. Include country of origin, production year, mint mark, series, grade, and the third-party grading service, if applicable (Bucki, 2020). Note the quantity of each type of coin, the date purchased, and the price originally paid.

Accessibility

The way you store your coin collection should allow easy access and retrieval of coins, facilitating viewing, handling, or adding new acquisitions. This ensures that the collection is not only secure but also functional for display and enjoyment.

Use storage solutions that allow you to easily remove and add coins. Consider the placement of storage containers in your home or a secure location that balances accessibility with security. For high-value collections, secure storage facilities with controlled access might be necessary to protect against theft or environmental damage (Petersen, 2022).

IMPLEMENTING SECURITY MEASURES

Implementing security measures ensures that your coin collection is not only stored in a safe environment but also protected against potential risks, providing peace of mind and safeguarding your valuable investment.

Safe Storage

A locked safe or vault at home offers a good level of security, especially if it's fireproof and burglar-resistant. For those with highly valuable collections, consider using a safe deposit box at a bank, which provides an added layer of security away from home. Ensure that the safe or vault is adequately secured to the building structure to prevent removal.

- **Home Safes:** Invest in a high-quality safe with a good fire rating and burglary resistance. Ensure it is anchored securely to prevent physical removal.
- **Safe Deposit Boxes:** For the highest security, a bank's safe deposit box offers strong protection against theft and is typically located in a vault with controlled access. (*What Is the Safest Way to Store Coins?*, 2022)

Insurance

Insuring your collection provides financial protection against loss, theft, or damage. Standard homeowner's insurance may not cover valuable coin collections adequately, so specialized coin insurance might be necessary. This type of insurance can cover the full value of the collection and is tailored to cover specific risks faced by coin collectors.

Assess the value of your collection and ensure your insurance coverage matches this value. It may be beneficial to consult with a professional appraiser and discuss your coverage needs with an insurance agent who understands collectibles.

Tightening Home Security

Enhance the security of the environment where your collection is stored. This includes robust physical security measures to prevent unauthorized access:

- **Locks and Entry Points:** Install high-quality locks, such as deadbolts on doors and windows. Consider upgrading to smart locks that provide alerts and remote monitoring capabilities.
- **Security Systems:** Employ a comprehensive home security system that includes alarms, motion detectors, and surveillance cameras. The visibility of security cameras can deter potential thieves.
- **Visibility and Lighting:** Use adequate exterior lighting to deter thieves. Motion-activated lights can surprise intruders, and maintaining a well-lit environment discourages unwanted visitors. (*Top 10 Home Security Tips*, 2022)

SUMMARY

- **Environmental Control:** Proper storage is vital to preserve both the appearance and value of coins. Moisture, temperature fluctuations, and exposure to air are significant factors that can deteriorate coins over time. Maintaining a controlled environment with humidity levels around 50% and temperatures below 75 degrees Fahrenheit is essential.

- **Protective Storage Materials:** Utilize inert and non-reactive storage materials to prevent chemical reactions that could damage the coins. Options include acid-free paper, archival-quality plastics, and inert metals like aluminum. These materials ensure that the coins are not only secure but also preserved in their original state without degradation.
- **Organized and Accessible Storage:** Implement an organized system for storing coins, which includes labeling and cataloging. Label coin holders, albums, or boxes with critical information like coin type, denomination, date, and mint mark for easy identification and retrieval. Maintain a detailed inventory that documents significant attributes and history of each coin.
- **Security Measures:** Secure storage options such as high-quality safes or safe deposit boxes protect against theft or loss. Additionally, enhancing home security with robust locks, surveillance systems, and adequate lighting around storage areas further safeguards the collection.
- **Insurance Coverage:** Consider obtaining insurance for the coin collection to cover potential losses from theft, damage, or other unforeseen incidents. Ensure that the insurance policy covers the full value of the collection and understand all aspects of the coverage to maximize protection.

CONCLUSION

Meticulous care in storing and organizing your coin collection is a necessity. Proper storage, carefully managing moisture, temperature, and air exposure, is crucial for keeping your coins looking good and valuable. Using containers that don't damage the coins and keeping the environment stable protect them from physical and chemical harm. It's just as important to organize your collection well, from picking the right storage options to keeping detailed records of each coin. Strong security and good insurance also play key roles in protecting your coins from any potential risks.

Looking ahead, our final chapter shifts our focus to the exciting realm of profit maximization in coin collecting. We will cover effective strategies for selling coins, optimizing profits, and navigating the often-overlooked tax implications. There is financial potential that your well-maintained collection holds, ensuring that your hobby not only preserves history but also enhances your financial future.

10

EXPLORING PROFIT OPPORTUNITY

Coin collecting, often perceived as a quiet, meticulous pursuit, occasionally unveils stories of unexpected fortunes and transformative journeys. Among these narratives, the saga of Robert Puddester stands out as particularly inspiring. An avid collector of coins related to the British East India Company, Puddester's lifelong passion not only culminated in a magnificent collection but also a lucrative return when he decided to auction it. His collection, meticulously assembled over 45 years, fetched nearly £2 million—a testament to the hidden potential in numismatics.

Robert Puddester's venture began and flourished with his move to India in 1983, where his professional assignments aligned serendipitously with his numismatic interests. Over the decades, Puddester's dedication to exploring and understanding the nuanced history of British Indian coinage allowed him to amass over 1,246 coins, making his collection one of the most comprehensive ever assembled. The sale of his coins, conducted by Noonans Mayfair, turned into a historic event, celebrated not just for the financial outcomes but for the sheer breadth and depth of the collection.

This chapter aims to explore how numismatics—often started as a hobby—can evolve into a significant investment opportunity. Through strategic acquisitions, understanding market dynamics, and a bit of historical luck, coin collecting can yield substantial financial rewards. As we delve deeper, we'll uncover the allure of rare coins, the intricacies of market demand, and strategic approaches to maximizing investment returns in the fascinating world of coin collecting.

THE POTENTIAL FOR PROFIT

By combining a passion for numismatics—the study and collection of currency—with strategic purchasing, collectors can turn a leisure activity into a lucrative investment.

The Allure of Rare Coins

Coin collecting offers significant financial incentives, primarily through the acquisition of rare and historically significant coins. Coins with high metal content, such as gold or silver, often maintain stable values and are less susceptible to market volatility. For instance, numismatic coins, which are valued for their rarity, condition, and historical importance, can fetch high prices on the market. The rarity and aesthetic appeal of a coin can significantly increase its value, making it a potentially high-return investment.

Understanding Market Demand

The market for rare coins has seen substantial growth, with an increase in spending on collectibles by over 20% in the past five years (Tips, 2022). This trend is driven by both seasoned collectors and new enthusiasts drawn to the historical and artistic value of coins. As demand grows, the value of rare coins tends to appreciate, especially those that are part of limited mintages or possess unique historical significance.

Educational and Networking Benefits

Engaging in coin collecting also offers educational benefits; collectors gain knowledge about history, economics, and the arts through their acquisitions. Moreover, the hobby provides opportunities to connect with other collectors and professionals in the field, creating a network that can offer advice, trade opportunities, and insights into market trends.

Risks and Considerations

While the potential for profit in coin collecting is considerable, it is not without risks. Understanding these risks is crucial for anyone considering coin collection as an investment.

Initial Investment and Market Fluctuations

The initial cost of acquiring rare or highly sought-after coins can be substantial. High-quality numismatic coins can cost thousands of dollars, and securing them often requires additional expenses, such as insurance and secure storage. Furthermore, while less volatile than other markets, the coin market can still experience fluctuations that affect the value of a collection.

Risk of Fraud and Theft

Investing in coins also involves risks of fraud and theft. The possibility of acquiring counterfeit coins or falling prey to unscrupulous dealers underscores the importance of dealing with reputable sellers and utilizing authentication services. Additionally, valuable collections attract the risk of theft, necessitating secure storage and insurance to protect the investment.

Long-Term Perspective

Coin collecting as an investment typically requires a long-term perspective. While some coins may appreciate quickly, most gains in value occur over many years. Collectors need to be patient and willing to hold onto their assets for extended periods to realize significant returns (Anderson, 2023).

STRATEGIES FOR PROFIT MAXIMIZATION

Maximizing profit in coin collection is not just about the luck of stumbling upon a valuable find; it involves strategic planning, thorough knowledge, and careful management of one's collection. Here are some practical strategies to enhance the profit potential of coin collecting:

Research and Education

Collectors must immerse themselves in the history, rarity, and value of coins to understand their history. Continuous learning through books, numismatic journals, and online platforms will enhance one's ability to identify profitable opportunities. As the market evolves, staying updated on trends and historical pricing can help collectors make informed decisions and spot underappreciated coins before they become widely recognized for their value.

To understand the history and value of coins, begin by subscribing to reputable numismatic journals such as *The Numismatist* and regularly visit websites like the Professional Coin Grading Service (PCGS). Learn to cross-reference the prices and details of coins using both *The Red Book* for U.S. coins and *The Standard Catalog of World Coins* for international varieties.

Starting Small

For beginners, the best approach is to start small. This strategy involves acquiring a few less expensive yet significant coins, which allows collectors to gain practical experience without the high stakes of more costly investments. Over time, this can gradually be scaled into a more diverse and valuable collection.

Start your collection with Lincoln Wheat Pennies, which are abundant and inexpensive. Focus on different mints and years that are less rare but still offer a historical glimpse into the past. This approach minimizes financial risk while building your numismatic skills.

Identifying Undervalued Coins

One key strategy is to identify coins that are undervalued relative to their historical importance or rarity. Coins that are overlooked in the market due to subtle variations or those from less popular series may offer significant growth potential as their value is recognized over time (Benvenuto, 2021). Collectors should look for coins where the supply is low but demand could increase, such as those from discontinued mints or coins with error marks that are rare but not yet highly sought after.

Regularly check completed auctions on platforms like Heritage Auctions to see the selling prices of coins. Compare these prices to current listings to spot undervalued coins. Pay special attention to coins from discontinued mints or those with error marks that have not yet been widely recognized.

Diversifying the Collection

Just as with other types of investments, diversification can mitigate risk in coin collecting. By acquiring a broad range of coins from different eras, countries, or types, collectors can protect themselves against fluctuations in the market for any single category. Diversification helps in balancing the portfolio so that the underperformance of some coins can be offset by the gains in others (*Strategies for Building Wealth with Coin Collections*, 2009). Expand your collection to include coins from various eras and countries. Start with modern U.S. quarters, then gradually include ancient coins such as Roman Denarii or Byzantine Bronzes.

Long-Term Perspective

Adopting a long-term perspective is essential for seeing substantial returns in numismatics. Investing in coins should be viewed as a long-term hold, where the value of coins generally appreciates over time. Collectors should focus on quality and rarity, acquiring coins that will likely be more desirable in the future. Avoiding the temptation to sell prematurely is crucial as many coins increase in value as they age and become more historic.

Focus on acquiring high-quality, rare coins that have historically appreciated over time. Avoid making impulsive decisions based on short-term market trends. Consider setting a goal to hold each coin for at least 5–10 years to maximize potential gains.

HOW TO SELL YOUR COINS

Assess Your Coin Collection

Start by organizing and cataloging your collection. Identify each coin, noting its denomination, year, mint mark, condition, and any unique features. Consider using a cataloging software or a spreadsheet for detailed records. This step is crucial for understanding the scope and value of your collection before making selling decisions.

Research Market Value

To determine the potential value of your coins, you need to research current market conditions. Use resources like the *Red Book*, online coin forums, auction results, and coin grading services to find out how much similar coins are selling for. This research will give you a ballpark figure of what to expect and help you set realistic prices.

Decide Where to Sell

You have several options when it comes to selling your coins:

- **Local Dealers:** Convenient for quick sales. Local dealers can offer instant cash, but may not always provide the best prices since they need to make a profit.
- **Coin Shows:** Great for reaching dedicated collectors. This option allows you to interact directly with multiple buyers and possibly get competitive offers.
- **Auction Houses:** Ideal for rare or high-value coins. Auctions can potentially fetch higher prices due to bidding wars. However, they come with fees and may take longer for you to receive payment.
- **Online Auctions or Marketplaces:** Platforms like eBay or Heritage Auctions reach a global audience. This method offers a broad market but requires you to handle listing, shipping, and customer interactions.

Prepare Your Coins for Sale

Ensure your coins are properly cleaned (if necessary and advisable), and present them attractively. Use appropriate holders or albums that protect the coins without obscuring any part of them. High-quality, clear photos are crucial for online sales.

List Your Coins

When listing your coins, provide detailed descriptions and clear, high-resolution images. Specify the condition of the coins, any historical significance, and other pertinent details. Accurate listings can help attract serious buyers and prevent disputes.

Market Your Coins

Utilize social media, coin forums, and other online platforms to reach potential buyers. If you're using an online marketplace or auction site, consider paying for premium listing options to increase visibility.

Negotiate Deals

Be prepared to engage in negotiations, armed with knowledge about each coin's worth. This will enable you to confidently navigate offers while ensuring you do not accept less than your set minimum price. Don't go below your minimum acceptable price.

Complete the Transaction

Once a sale agreement is reached, ensure all terms are clearly communicated. Use secure payment methods and provide prompt, insured shipping. If selling in person, arrange meetings in safe, public locations. Ensure all terms of the sale are clear and agreed upon. Use secure, traceable payment methods and ship the coins insured to protect both parties. If dealing in person, choose a safe, public venue for the exchange to ensure security.

TAX CONSIDERATIONS

The IRS categorizes coin collections and precious metals as collectibles. When buying, selling, trading, or inheriting such items, certain tax implications come into play. If you sell a collectible, such as coins, at a profit, the gain may be subject to capital gains tax. This is true whether the coins were held as a part of a collection or as an investment.

Types of Taxes That May Apply

- **Capital Gains Tax:** This is the tax on the profit made from selling your coins for more than their purchase price. If held for more than one year, collectibles are taxed at a maximum rate of 28% (Moskowitz, 2019). However, if sold within a year, the gains are taxed as ordinary income, which could be higher depending on your tax bracket.
- **Sales Tax:** This tax is imposed on the sale of coins and varies by location. Not all states charge sales tax on coins, and rates can differ widely.
- **Inheritance Tax:** If coins are inherited, they are subject to estate or inheritance taxes depending on the laws of the state where the decedent was resident. The basis of the coins for the beneficiary is stepped up to the market value at the time of the original owner's death, which could affect the gain when the coins are later sold.
- **State and Local Taxes:** These may include additional taxes on sales, transfers, or holdings of collectibles, depending on local laws.

Reporting Requirements

For income earned from the sale of coins, the IRS requires detailed record-keeping. Collectors must maintain records of the purchase price, any associated costs, and the selling price of each coin. This information is crucial for accurately reporting capital gains or losses on IRS Form 8949 and Schedule D of your tax return (Jones, 2023b). Proper documentation includes sales receipts, purchase invoices, and possibly appraisals, especially for high-value items.

SUMMARY

- **Investment Potential Through Numismatics:** Coin collecting merges passion with investment, turning numismatics into a potentially lucrative venture. By strategically acquiring rare and historically significant coins, collectors can transform their hobby into a serious investment opportunity.
- **Market Demand and Value Appreciation:** The market for rare coins is growing, driven by both seasoned collectors and new enthusiasts. Coins, especially those with historical and aesthetic significance, often appreciate in value over time, bolstered by limited mintages and unique attributes.
- **Educational and Networking Opportunities:** Coin collecting offers more than financial benefits; it provides educational insights into history, economics, and the arts. Additionally, it opens networking opportunities with other collectors and experts, enhancing both knowledge and investment possibilities.

- **Risks and Strategic Considerations:** While promising, coin collecting comes with risks such as market fluctuations, potential fraud, and theft. Strategic planning, thorough research, and careful management are essential for maximizing profits, including starting with less expensive coins and gradually diversifying the collection.
- **Selling Strategy and Tax Implications:** Successfully selling coins involves meticulous cataloging, understanding market values, and choosing the right sales platform. Collectors must also be aware of tax implications on profits from sales, including capital gains and sales taxes, and ensure they keep detailed records for tax purposes.

CONCLUSION

Coin collecting offers financial benefits, and the key takeaways from this exploration include the profit potential inherent in collecting rare and historically important coins, the necessity of understanding market dynamics, and the importance of strategic purchasing. Moreover, we have outlined the educational and networking opportunities that collecting offers, enriching one's knowledge and creating valuable connections within the numismatic community.

This chapter has also highlighted the inherent risks of coin collecting, such as market fluctuations and the potential for fraud, emphasizing the need for careful planning and informed decision-making. By engaging with these insights, readers are equipped to navigate the complexities of the numismatic market, enhance the value of their collections, and avoid common pitfalls.

As we close this final chapter, take a moment to appreciate the distance you've traveled in this numismatic journey. Whether you started as a curious novice or a seasoned collector seeking to refine your craft, you now stand equipped with the knowledge and strategies to enhance your collecting experience and potentially profit from your passion.

Congratulations on completing this exploration into the world of coin collecting. Armed with your newfound insights and techniques, the future of your numismatic journey is not just a continuation of a hobby but a pathway to discovery and potential financial reward. Here's to your success and the endless possibilities that lie ahead in the fascinating realm of coins!

CONNECT WITH NEW COLLECTORS!

There is so much joy to be found in coin collecting, in preserving the history of each coin you acquire... and this is your chance to give the gift of that joy to new collectors.

Simply by sharing your honest opinion of this book and a little about your own journey with coin collecting, you'll help connect new readers with this rich and rewarding endeavor.

Thank you so much for your support. Information is at its most powerful when it's shared, and your words make a huge difference.

Scan the QR code below to leave a review:

CONCLUSION

You might start your coin collecting journey with just a casual interest and some spare change. By using a guide like *Coin Collecting for Beginners*, you can transform that casual interest into a knowledgeable pursuit. You now have the essential information you need to identify valuable coins, understand their historical context, and properly care for your collection. Like the coins from my grandfather's collection that sparked my interest, each coin you acquire could be the key to unlocking a new piece of history.

I designed this guide to teach you how to collect and preserve coins for future generations. I hope to have also fostered a passion for history. As digital forms of currency gain popularity, the importance of this tactile connection to our past becomes even more critical. The next time you hold a coin, think about how it uniquely embodies the intersection of history, art, and commerce right in the palm of your hand. Cataloguing and preserving these aspects of our culture is more important now than ever.

As a coin collector, you carry the responsibility of safeguarding history through the preservation of currency. As stewards of these tiny artifacts, you are uniquely positioned to protect and pass on the stories and lessons from past civilizations. In an era where digital currencies are becoming more prevalent, physical coins serve as tangible links to different epochs and cultures. Furthermore, your growing expertise empowers you to debunk common myths about coin collecting, such as the misconceptions that all old coins are exceedingly valuable or that numismatics is merely financial speculation. By educating others with accurate information, you help promote a deeper appreciation for this engaging hobby and its historical significance. This role enhances the importance of your efforts, reinforcing the value of each coin not just as a collector's item, but as a piece of history that tells the rich story of human civilization.

You must ensure that these coins are preserved not just for personal enjoyment or financial investment, but as cultural heirlooms for future generations. This involves meticulous care in handling, storing, and documenting your collection. Beyond personal care, you can engage in educational outreach, sharing your knowledge and passion with others to foster a broader appreciation. This engagement helps ensure that the historical and artistic value of coins is recognized and preserved beyond mere monetary worth. By doing so, you contribute to a deeper understanding of history and heritage through the art of numismatics.

Keep in mind these key points from the book:

- **Accessible Hobby:** Coin collecting is an accessible and enjoyable hobby that welcomes everyone. You don't need

extensive financial resources or specialized knowledge to start your own collection.
- **Historical and Cultural Appreciation:** As you collect coins, you're also collecting pieces of history. Each coin connects you to past civilizations, allowing you to explore their economic, cultural, and political landscapes.
- **Educational Value:** This hobby isn't just about accumulating coins; it's a learning journey. You'll gain deeper insights into the art and science of numismatics, enhancing your understanding of different eras and their unique characteristics.
- **Community and Connection:** Coin collecting brings enthusiasts together, creating a vibrant community. You'll have opportunities to share your knowledge, trade coins, and celebrate your passion for numismatics with others who are just as passionate.
- **Potential for Investment:** While it may not be the main reason you start collecting, there's potential for investment. The value of certain coins may appreciate over time, depending on their rarity and condition, offering you not only a hobby but a potential financial benefit.

Without this guide, you might miss recognizing rare coins, misjudge their value, or damage valuable pieces due to improper handling. The structured advice provided helps you avoid common pitfalls that many beginners encounter, such as overspending on common coins or falling for scams involving counterfeit pieces.

Savor the rich experiences this hobby offers—from historical exploration to community engagement and potential financial rewards. It opens up a world of possibilities, all accessible to you. Use what you've learned from this book to advance your collecting. Continue learning and discovering in the world of coins—there's much more ahead! If you've felt the spark of curiosity and the excitement of discovery through coin collecting, know that your adventure is far from over.

As you delve deeper into the world of numismatics, your appreciation for each piece in your collection will grow, knowing that behind every coin is a story that bridges generations. You are now connected to the rich historical and cultural significance of numismatics.

I aim to make your hobby as rewarding and enriching as possible. If this book has guided you well, consider sharing your experience. Leave a review, spread the word, and perhaps inspire another to begin their own numismatic journey. Just as coins pass from hand to hand, so too can the knowledge and passion for this enduring pursuit.

QUIZ

Take this final quiz to evaluate your understanding of the subjects explored in the concluding chapters of the book. Reflect on the historical insights, the detailed nuances of coin collecting, and your personal learning journey throughout.

UNDERSTANDING COIN COLLECTING BASICS

Multiple Choice Questions

1. Which grading system is used globally for coins?

- A) Numeric system
- B) Pictorial scale
- C) Alphanumeric scale
- D) Binary system

2. What aspect of a coin does not influence its grade?

- A) Design
- B) Color
- C) Diameter
- D) Wear

3. Where is the mint mark located on a U.S. coin?

- A) On the obverse, typically below the date
- B) On the reverse, near the top
- C) Along the rim
- D) Embedded within the design

4. Which of the following is true about handling coins?

- A) Coins should be stored touching each other to save space
- B) Cotton gloves should be used to avoid skin oils
- C) It's best to handle coins in direct sunlight
- D) Coins are best cleaned with tap water

5. What is the purpose of a coin slab?

- A) Decoration
- B) To prevent coins from clinking
- C) Protection and authentication
- D) To increase the weight of the coin

6. What is the main disadvantage of using PVC holders for coins?

- A) They are expensive
- B) They can corrode the coin
- C) They are too large
- D) They decrease the coin's value

7. Which feature on a coin is most likely to have incuse elements?

- A) The edge
- B) The field
- C) The rim
- D) The inscription

8. Which condition is considered perfect in coin grading?

- A) MS-50
- B) MS-60
- C) MS-70
- D) MS-100

9. What is the significance of a coin's patina?

- A) It can protect the coin from further corrosion
- B) It decreases the coin's value
- C) It makes the coin easier to counterfeit
- D) It is purely decorative

10. Which method is not recommended for researching coin values?

- A) Consulting a numismatic magazine
- B) Asking a friend
- C) Looking up online auctions
- D) Checking a coin value guidebook

11. How does one typically obtain proof coins?

- A) Through general circulation
- B) By special order through the mint
- C) Finding them in change
- D) Winning them in lotteries

12. What is a coin's 'field'?

- A) The raised design on the surface
- B) The flat background area
- C) The serrated edge
- D) The part that shows wear first

13. What does reeded edge on a coin help prevent?

- A) Oxidation
- B) Counterfeiting
- C) Bending
- D) Discoloration

14. Which material is least likely to be used for storing coins?

- A) Mylar
- B) Silicon
- C) Acrylic
- D) Cardboard

15. What is NOT a characteristic of bullion coins?

- A) They are used as legal tender
- B) They are valued based on their metal content
- C) They are typically not well-designed
- D) They may appreciate in value based on metal prices

16. Which is not a typical characteristic of ancient coins?

- A) They are made of precious metals
- B) They have no face value
- C) They feature the likeness of historical figures
- D) They often show high levels of craftsmanship

17. Why are coin grades important to investors?

- A) They indicate the potential resale value
- B) They suggest the age of the coin
- C) They determine the coin's minting location
- D) They provide information about the coin's previous owners

18. What type of cleaning is most harmful to coins?

    - A) Light brushing with a soft brush
    - B) Dipping in acetone
    - C) Gentle washing with distilled water
    - D) Abrasive scrubbing

19. Which term describes a coin minted incorrectly by the mint?

    - A) Proof
    - B) Bullion
    - C) Error
    - D) Commemorative

20. What does the term 'exonumia' refer to?

    - A) The collection of foreign coins
    - B) The study of coin edges
    - C) The collection of coin-like objects
    - D) The exchange of coins at auctions

True/False Questions

1. All coins with numismatic value are old. (True/False)
2. Bullion coins are primarily collected for their aesthetic designs. (True/False)
3. Coins should be cleaned regularly to maintain their value. (True/False)
4. A coin's weight never changes over time. (True/False)
5. Historical coins can be a good investment. (True/False)
6. Coin grading can only be performed by experts. (True/False)

7. Numismatics is the study of paper money only. (True/False)
8. PVC is safe for long-term coin storage. (True/False)
9. All commemorative coins are considered legal tender. (True/False)
10. The obverse of a coin is typically called the "heads" side. (True/False)

Fill-in-the-Blank Questions

1. Coins with a high level of _____ detail are often valued higher.
2. The _____ is typically where the coin's mint mark is found.
3. Coins graded MS-70 are considered to be in _____ condition.
4. _____ is a common material used in coin capsules.
5. The design on the reverse of a coin often includes _____ elements.
6. Coins made purely for collectors are known as _____ coins.
7. _____ indicates the type of metal used to make the coin.
8. A coin's _____ can affect its grade and overall value.
9. _____ coins are those that have never been circulated.
10. To prevent damage, coins should not be exposed to excessive _____.

ANSWERS

Multiple Choice

1. A, 2. C, 3. A, 4. B, 5. C, 6. B, 7. D, 8. C, 9. A, 10. B, 11. B, 12. B, 13. B, 14. B, 15. C, 16. B, 17. A, 18. D, 19. C, 20. C

True/False

1. False, 2. False, 3. False, 4. False, 5. True, 6. False, 7. False, 8. False, 9. True, 10. True

Fill-in-the-Blank

1. relief, 2. obverse, 3. perfect, 4. acrylic, 5. historical, 6. proof, 7. composition, 8. patina, 9. uncirculated, 10. humidity.

GRADING SCALE FOR QUIZ

- **36-40 correct answers: Excellent (90-100%)**
  - Exceptional understanding of the material with high proficiency demonstrated.

- **32-35 correct answers: Very Good (80-89%)**
  - Strong grasp of the content with minor areas for improvement.

- **26-31 correct answers: Good (65-79%)**

  ○ Solid comprehension, though some concepts may need further review.

- **20-25 correct answers: Satisfactory (50-64%)**

  ○ Adequate understanding, but further study and review are necessary.

- **14-19 correct answers: Needs Improvement (35-49%)**

  ○ Partial understanding with significant gaps in knowledge.

- **0-13 correct answers: Unsatisfactory (0-34%)**

  ○ Poor understanding, substantial improvement and additional study required.

REFERENCES

Allcot, D. (2023, October 26). *Looking to buy or sell valuable coins or bills? 7 scam red flags to watch for*. Yahoo Finance. https://finance.yahoo.com/news/looking-buy-sell-valuable-coins-152206625.html

The anatomy of a coin. (2018, December 11). American Mint. https://www.americanmint.com/the-anatomy-of-a-coin

The anatomy of a coin explained. (2022, January 7). All about Coins. https://www.allaboutcoins.co.uk/start-collecting/coin-collecting-basics/the-anatomy-of-a-coin-explained/

Anderson, S. (2023, August 20). *Coin collection as a long-term investment: The ros and cons*. Your Coffee Break. https://www.yourcoffeebreak.co.uk/money/26338797266/coin-collection-as-a-long-term-investment-the-pros-and-cons/

Bautista-González, M. A. (2023, February 1). *United States: Coin production and circulation*. Cash Essentials. https://cashessentials.org/united-states-coin-production-and-circulation/

Benvenuto, M. (2021, February 23). *Undervalued beauties in different U.S. coin series*. Numismatic News. https://www.numismaticnews.net/collecting-101/undervalued-beauties-in-different-u-s-coin-series

Bozarth, V., & Ferguson, M. (2021, October 13). *Coin market trends: Demand for rare coins continues soaring*. PCGS. https://www.pcgs.com/news/coin-market-trends-demand-for-rare-coins-continues-soaring

The brief history of world coins. (2017, March 14). Coinappraiser.com. https://coinappraiser.com/brief-history-world-coins/

Bucki, J. (2020, November 17). *The easy way to catalog your coin collection*. The Spruce Crafts. https://www.thesprucecrafts.com/cataloging-your-coin-collection-768293

Bucki, J. (2021, December 30). *Discover 6 reasons to start collecting coins*. The Spruce Crafts. https://www.thesprucecrafts.com/reasons-to-start-collecting-coins-4589015

Bucki, J. (2022a, April 27). *8 coin holders for your collection*. The Spruce Crafts. https://www.thesprucecrafts.com/types-of-coin-holders-768327

Bucki, J. (2022b, September 21). *How to detect counterfeit coins*. The Spruce Crafts. https://www.thesprucecrafts.com/how-to-detect-counterfeit-coins-4163525

Bucki, J. M. (2023, January 20). *Coin collecting 301 - collecting coins by type vs. series*.

https://www.greysheet.com/news/story/coin-collecting-301-collecting-coins-by-type-vs-series

Chi, Clifford. "15 Inspiring Storytelling Quotes to Help You Move an Audience." HubSpot Blog | Marketing, Sales, Agency, and Customer Success Content. Last modified July 24, 2019. https://blog.hubspot.com/marketing/storytelling-quotes

Choosing the right storage to protect coin values. (2014, March 23). Grand Rapids Coins. https://www.grandrapidscoins.com/choosing-the-right-storage-to-protect-coin-values/

Circulating coins. (n.d.). U.S. Mint. https://www.usmint.gov/learn/coin-and-medal-programs/circulating-coins

Coin cleaning: Mechanical, chemical & electrochemical Methods. (2022, September 5). PSIBERG. https://psiberg.com/coin-cleaning/

Coin collecting guide. (n.d.). Chards. https://www.chards.co.uk/guides/numismatic-information-and-coin-collecting-guides

Coin collecting: a beginner's guide to the hobby of coin collecting. (2016, September 7). London Mint Office. https://www.londonmintoffice.org/learn/coin-collecting-a-beginners-guide-the-hobby-of-coin-collecting

Coin grading: Grade can help determine coin value. (2022, May 24). AMPEX. https://learn.apmex.com/learning-guide/coin-collecting/coin-grading-grade-can-help-determine-coin-value/

Coin minting technology throughout the ages: Ancients to today. (2019, September 15). Provident Metals. https://www.providentmetals.com/knowledge-center/collectible-coins/history-coin-minting-technology.html

Coin production. (2024). U.S. Mint. https://www.usmint.gov/learn/production-process/coin-production

Coin shows and auctions: A collector's guide. (2023, July 12). Coincollecting.com. https://www.coincollecting.com/coin-shows-and-auctions-a-collector-s-guide

Coins at estate sales. (2022, July 21). Estate Pros. https://goestatepros.com/estate-sale-tips/coins-at-estate-sales/

Coins authenticity verification. (n.d.). Banco de México. https://www.banxico.org.mx/banknotes-and-coins/coins-authenticity-verificati.html

A complete coin grading guide for all investing skill levels. (2024, January 15). Oxford Gold Group. https://www.oxfordgoldgroup.com/articles/coin-grading-guide/#The_Three_Coin-Grading_Buckets

Davidson, M. (2023, March 28). *Coin grading chart: Determine the condition and value of your coins.* Valuable U.S Coins. https://www.valuableuscoins.com/coin-grading-chart/

Discover British coin grading: Your ultimate guide. (2023, November 30). The Coin

Expert. https://thecoinexpert.co.uk/blog/british-coin-gradwzing-understanding-the-value-and-quality-of-coins/

Four easy steps to becoming a coin collector. (2015, January 3). Liberty Coin & Currency. https://libertycoinandcurrency.com/blog/four-easy-steps-to-becoming-a-coin-collector/

4 Reasons Why It's Important To Track Your Goals And Milestones. (2022, May 6). Nucleusapp.io. https://nucleusapp.io/productivity-articles/why-its-important-to-track-your-goals-and-milestones/

Garrett, J. (2022, September 29). *What to do when there are no price guides.* NGC. https://www.ngccoin.com/news/article/10701/

Garrett, J. (2023, February 2). *The importance of learning to grade coins.* GovMint.com. https://www.govmint.com/coin-authority/post/the-importance-of-learning-to-grade-coins

Golino, L. (n.d.). *Coin forums and social media sites can be useful.* CoinWorld. https://www.coinworld.com/voices/louis-golino/coin_forums_and_soci.html

The grading process. (2024). Independent Coin Graders. https://www.icgcoin.com/about-us/the-grading-process/

Headley, S. (2021a, January 31). *Which part is the obverse of a coin?* The Spruce Crafts. https://www.thesprucecrafts.com/obverse-of-a-coin-768467

Headley, S. (2021b, October 30). *7 things you should never do to your coins!* The Spruce Crafts. https://www.thesprucecrafts.com/top-ways-to-ruin-your-coins-768318

Headley, S. (2022a, January 19). *This is the difference between the coin's edge and rim.* The Spruce Crafts. https://www.thesprucecrafts.com/edge-vs-rim-768375

Headley, S. (2022b, June 29). *Proof coins explained.* The Spruce Crafts. https://www.thesprucecrafts.com/what-is-a-proof-coin-768471

The history of coins. (n.d.). Certified Coin Consultants Inc. https://certifiedcoinconsultants.com/pages/the-history-of-coins

Hockley, M. (2024, April 1). *How to start a coin collection in 2024 in 4 simple steps!* Silverpicker. https://thesilverpicker.com/how-to-start-a-coin-collection/#Step_3_Set_a_Budget

How much is your collection worth: The benefits of coin appraisal. (n.d.). Unique Gold & Diamonds. https://www.uniquegoldanddiamonds.com/pages/how-much-is-your-collection-worth-the-benefits-of-coin-appraisal

How not to clean coins + tips for cleaning coins properly. (2013, April 9). U.S. Coin Guide. https://coins.thefuntimesguide.com/how-to-clean-coins/

How to authenticate coins in your coin collection. (n.d.). Antique Marks. https://antique-marks.com/how-to-authenticate-coins.html

How to store coins - full guide. (n.d.). Preservation Equipment Ltd. https://www.preservationequipment.com/Blog/Blog-Posts/How-to-store-coins-full-guide

How to store coins safely: A complete guide. (2022, September 24). The Oxford Gold Group. https://www.oxfordgoldgroup.com/articles/how-to-store-coins-safely/#What_Factors_Can_Damage_or_Tarnish_Valuable_Coins

How to store coins safely: A precious metals guide. (2023, June 22). Learn about Gold. https://learnaboutgold.com/blog/how-to-store-coins-safely/#Why_Is_Proper_Coin_Storage_Important

How to submit. (n.d.). NGC. https://www.ngccoin.com/submit/how-to-submit/

Is it important to grade your coins? (n.d.). GMR Gold. https://www.gmrgold.com/blog/is-it-important-to-grade-your-coins-.cfm

Jobes, N. (2022, January 20). *Coin collecting guide - everything you need to know.* The Collectors Guides Centre. https://grandcollector.com/coin-collecting-guide

Jones, N. (2023a, March 23). *5 tips on buying coin collecting lamp.* The Collectors Guides Centre. https://grandcollector.com/coin-collecting-lamp/

Jones, N. (2023b, May 8). *What you need to know about taxes for coin collection.* The Collectors Guides Centre. https://grandcollector.com/taxes-for-coin-collection/

Jones, N. (2024, January 30). *Is collecting coins an expensive hobby?* The Collectors Guides Centre. https://grandcollector.com/is-collecting-coins-an-expensive-hobby/

Lyons, K. (2024, April 2). *How to clean old coins (without damaging them).* Cleaner Digs. https://cleanerdigs.com/how-to-clean-old-coins/#How_to_Clean_Old_Coins_5_DIY_Methods

McMorrow-Hernandez, J. (n.d.). *Why you shouldn't clean your coins.* Coin Values. https://coinvalues.com/library/why-you-shouldnt-clean-your-coins#google_vignette

McMorrow-Hernandez, J. (2019, July 17). *The future of coin collecting looks bright.* The Coin Values Blog. https://coinvalues.com/blog/the-future-of-coin-collecting-looks-bright

McMorrow-Hernandez, J. (2021, September 28). *In coins, what does incuse mean?* Professional Coin Grading Services. https://www.pcgs.com/news/in-coins-what-does-incuse-mean

McVicker, A. (2022, July 1). *The people behind the coins: Coin artists and engravers.* ModernCoinMart. https://moderncoinmart.com/coin-artists-and-engravers/

Meredith, S. (2020, September 21). *How coins are made: Bringing coins into circulation.* United States Mint. https://www.usmint.gov/news/inside-the-mint/how-coins-are-made-bringing-coins-into-circulation

Mint marks. (n.d.). United States Mint. https://www.usmint.gov/learn/collecting-basics/mint-marks

Mints of the world. (n.d.). Mint Industry. https://mintindustry.com/about/global-mint-industry/mints-of-the-world/

Moskowitz, D. (2019). *How collectibles are taxed*. Investopedia. https://www.investopedia.com/articles/personal-finance/061715/how-are-collectibles-taxed.asp

The NGC introduces a new 10-Point grading scale for coins. (2023, February 20). Provident Metals. https://blog.providentmetals.com/the-ngc-introduces-a-new-10-point-grading-scale-for-coins.htm

Passy, C. (2021, October 14). *With prices for some rarities in the millions of dollars, collectible coins are becoming a hot item*. MarketWatch. https://www.marketwatch.com/story/why-so-many-people-even-crypto-fans-are-buying-rare-coins-prices-are-at-never-before-seen-highs-11642106485

Petersen, M. (2022, March 16). *Coin collection storage*. Safe Haven Private Vaults. https://safehavenvaults.com/be-mindful-of-these-three-things-when-storing-rare-coins/

Photos of damaged coins - these are the kinds of coins to avoid collecting! (2022, February 23). U.S. Coins Guide. https://coins.thefuntimesguide.com/damaged_coins/

Reverse side of a coin. (n.d.). Bullion by Post. https://www.bullionbypost.co.uk/index/collectible-coins/reverse-side-of-a-coin/

Sayles, W. (2024, January 31). *Coin collecting | History, value & types*. Brittanica. https://www.britannica.com/topic/coin-collecting#ref237312

Sepanek, E. (2024, February 9). *Coin damage vs mint errors: Spotting the difference*. Scottsdale Bullion & Coin. https://www.sbcgold.com/blog/coin-damage-vs-mint-errors-spotting-the-difference/

Services. (n.d.). ANACS. https://anacs.com/services/

Shopping and paying safely online. (n.d.). MaPS. https://www.moneyhelper.org.uk/en/everyday-money/banking/shop-safely-online

6 famous coin engravers and designers in US history. (2019, September 15). Provident Metals. https://www.providentmetals.com/knowledge-center/collectible-coins/famous-american-coin-engravers.html

6 rules for properly handling your precious metal coins. (2019, September 15). Provident Metals. https://www.providentmetals.com/knowledge-center/collectible-coins/handling-precious-metal-coins.html

Spurrier, L. (2021, August 5). *5 key factors that influence coin values*. American Numismatic Association. https://blog.money.org/coin-collecting/5-factors-influence-coin-values

Spurrier, L. (2022, August 17). *Purchasing coins online*. American Numismatic Association. https://blog.money.org/coin-collecting/purchasing-coins-online

Stevens, J. (2023a, June 5). *Mastering coin handling etiquette: Essential techniques for coin collectors*. All My Treasures. https://allmytreasures.com/coin-handling-etiquette/#Importance_of_coin_handling_etiquette

Stevens, J. (2023b, June 20). *Unlock the secrets of coin valuation: A guide for coin collectors.* All My Treasures. https://allmytreasures.com/coin-valuation/#Importance_of_Coin_Valuation_for_Coin_Collectors

Strategies for building wealth with coin collections. (2009, December 7). Gainesville Coins. https://www.gainesvillecoins.com/blog/strategies-for-investing-in-coin-collections

Sullivan, J. (2022, January 10). *Deciphering mint errors versus post-mint damage.* PCGS. https://www.pcgs.com/news/deciphering-mint-errors-versus-post-mint-damage

10 coin collections you can assemble for under $100. (2021, September 15). Franklin Mint. https://franklinmint.com/blogs/coin-collecting-101/10-coin-collections-you-can-assemble-for-under-100

Thorne, M. (2023, June 16). *Why you should learn to grade for yourself.* Numismatic News. https://www.numismaticnews.net/collecting-101/why-you-should-learn-to-grade-for-yourself

Tips, S. B. (2022, December 15). *Is coin collecting a profitable business idea?* Start Business Tips. https://startbusinesstips.com/is-coin-collecting-a-profitable-business-idea/

Top 10 home security tips for coin collectors. (2022, May 23). COINage Magazine. https://www.coinagemag.com/home-security-for-collectors/

Turner, J. (2020, March 2). *Error or variety?* PCGS. https://www.pcgs.com/news/coin-error-or-variety

Types of coin damage and mint errors. (2023, August 21). American Bullion. https://www.americanbullion.com/types-of-coin-damage-and-mint-errors/

U.S. Mint artistic sculpting process. (2021, June 29). United States Mint. https://www.usmint.gov/learn/production-process/sculpting

Using authentication and grading services. (n.d.). EBay. https://www.ebay.com/help/terms-conditions/default/using-authentication-grading-services?id=4659

What are bullion coins? (2021, October 7). Coincollecting.com. https://www.coincollecting.com/what-are-bullion-coins

What is a coin? (2023, March 1). U.S. Hedge Funds. https://ushedgefunds.com/currencies/what-is-a-coin/

What is a mint? Definition, U.S. Mint history and statistics. (2021, February 25). Investopedia. https://www.investopedia.com/terms/m/mint.asp

What is coin grading and why? (n.d.). PCGS. https://www.pcgs.com/whatiscoingrading

What is the safest way to store coins? (2022, May 23). COINage Magazine. https://www.coinagemag.com/what-is-the-safest-way-to-store-coins/

What is your coin collecting goal? (2022, March 19). Reddit. https://www.reddit.com/r/coins/comments/thtuqj/what_is_your_coin_collecting_goal/

What to do with mutilated currency. (2017, August 21). Great American Coin Company. https://www.greatamericancoincompany.com/a/info/blog/what-to-do-with-mutilated-currency

What's the difference between being a numismatist & a coin collector? (2018, April 10). U.S. Coins Guide. https://coins.thefuntimesguide.com/numismatist/

Whipps, H. (2007, November 16). *The profound history of coins.* Live Science. https://www.livescience.com/2058-profound-history-coins.html

Why do you collect coins? (2004, November 1). EBay Community. https://community.ebay.com/t5/U-S-Coin-Collectors/Why-Do-You-Collect-Coins/m-p/5340225

Why is it important to handle coins properly? (2015, March 4). Rocky Mountain Coin. https://rmcoin.com/blog/7-rules-for-handling-rare-coins/

IMAGE REFERENCES

Figure 1. cottonbro studio. (2020, February 25). *Gold and Silver Round Coins* [Image]. Pexels. https://www.pexels.com/photo/gold-and-silver-round-coins-3943719/

Figure 2. papazachariasa. (2020, January 22). *Coins* [Image]. Pixabay. https://pixabay.com/photos/coins-ancient-roman-money-old-4786028/

Figure 3. WikiImages. (2013, January 3). *Coin Dollar Currency Money* [Image]. Pixabay. https://pixabay.com/photos/coin-dollar-currency-money-67725/

Figure 4. Monstera Production. (2021, March 28). *Anonymous person with magnifying glass over world map of coins* [Image]. Pexels. https://www.pexels.com/photo/anonymous-person-with-magnifying-glass-over-world-map-of-coins-7412089/

Figure 5. stevepb. (2014, September 18). *Vernier Caliper Measuring Instrument* [Image]. Pixabay. https://pixabay.com/photos/vernier-caliper-measuring-instrument-452987/

Figure 6. PIX1861. (2017, May 1). *Gold Coin Gold Gold Ducat* [Image]. Pixabay. https://pixabay.com/photos/gold-coin-gold-gold-ducat-2269848/

Figure 7. Jimmy Chan. (2018, July 13). *Round Silver-colored Coin on Brown Printer Paper* [Image]. Pexels. https://www.pexels.com/photo/round-silver-colored-coin-on-brown-printer-paper-1235972/

Figure 8. A_Different_Perspective. (2016, May 19). *Silver Coin Edge Embossing Coin* [Image]. Pixabay. https://pixabay.com/photos/silver-coin-edge-embossing-coin-1404320/

Figure 9. Todd Trapani. (2018, September 26). *Silver Coin* [Image]. Pexels. https://www.pexels.com/photo/silver-coin-1461996/

Figure 10. mattyh. (2018, February 18). *Isolated Currency Metallic Idaho* [Image]. Pixabay. https://pixabay.com/photos/isolated-currency-metallic-idaho-3164330/

Figure 11. Jimmy Chan. (2018, July 13). *Round Silver-colored Liberty Coin* [Image]. Pexels. https://www.pexels.com/photo/round-silver-colored-liberty-coin-1235971/

Figure 12. Lewis Ashton. (2022, November 20). *Single Collectible Coin* [Image]. Pexels. https://www.pexels.com/photo/single-collectible-coin-14506398/

Figure 13. cottonbro studio. (2020, February 25). *Persons Leg With Silver Round*

Coins [Image]. Pexels. https://www.pexels.com/photo/persons-leg-with-silver-round-coins-3943750/

Figure 14. Yuri Krupenin. (2021, December 10). *A Close-up of a Person Playing a Board Game* [Image]. Unsplash. https://unsplash.com/photos/a-close-up-of-a-person-playing-a-board-game-S2FVm0tOv1w

Figure 15. Zlaťáky.cz. (2021, May 25). *Blue and Gold Can on White Table* [Image]. Unsplash. https://unsplash.com/photos/blue-and-gold-can-on-white-table-Bn77cbbbqOQ

Figure 16. CoinMaster123. (2019, March 15). *Ancient Coins on Display* [Image]. Pixabay. https://pixabay.com/photos/ancient-coins-collection-4053852/

Figure 17. NumisArt. (2021, August 10). *Old Coin Collection* [Image]. Pexels. https://www.pexels.com/photo/old-coin-collection-7124851/

Figure 18. Lydia Montague. (2022, January 5). *Rare Gold Coins* [Image]. Unsplash. https://unsplash.com/photos/rare-gold-coins-4839498/

Figure 19. SilverTreasures. (2020, October 14). *Vintage Coins on Wooden Table* [Image]. Pixabay. https://pixabay.com/photos/vintage-coins-wooden-table-3629472/

Figure 20. Xavier Blythe. (2018, July 23). *Collector Displaying Coins* [Image]. Pexels. https://www.pexels.com/photo/collector-displaying-coins-2535478/

Made in the USA
Las Vegas, NV
03 February 2025